Praise for **Crossing the Swamp**

Crossing the Swamp is an inspiring memoir that takes readers on a captivating journey through the highs and lows of John Shen's parallel entrepreneur's life. This book offers valuable insights and wisdom for aspiring entrepreneurs looking to navigate the complex world of business development. I highly recommend this book.

—Fiona Ma, California State Treasurer

From its gripping start to its motivating finish, *Crossing the Swamp* is a must-read for entrepreneurs at any stage. John Shen shares his 20 years of business experience to help us overcome the challenges business (and life) will surely throw our way! Whether you are a veteran or a novice, you will find the tools you need and the inspiration to use them.

—Michael Houlihan and Bonnie Harvey, Founders of Barefoot Wines, *New York Times* Bestselling Authors of *The Barefoot Spirit*

What sets *Crossing the Swamp* apart from other books on entrepreneurship are its clear strategies for adapting to challenges and change, based on Shen's real-life business experience . . . Businesses, libraries, and entrepreneurs seeking concrete advice on common obstacles to entrepreneuring and how to overcome them must have *Crossing the Swamp* in their collections.

—D. Donovan, Midwest Book Review, Senior Reviewer

John Shen offers down-to-earth, practical, insightful, and comprehensive lessons learned along his fascinating twenty-year journey from a Chinese immigrant to a multiple national award-winning parallel entrepreneur of five companies in this must-read book for entrepreneurs . . . .

—Imran Currim, Executive Director, Beall Center for Innovation and Entrepreneurship, and Distinguished Professor of Marketing, UC Irvine Paul Merage School of Business

In *Crossing the Swamp,* John Shen shares the story of his own successful parallel ventures while presenting a roadmap of eight key elements which are vital for any parallel entrepreneur to adopt to avoid pitfalls and achieve success. John outlines these points while sharing the ups and downs of his personal journey with brutal honesty and clarity. This approach is why I believe *Crossing the Swamp* is not only critical for the parallel entrepreneur but greatly beneficial to any modern entrepreneur or student of business.

— Bruce Thompson, California politician

A well-constructed memoir/business guide with a special focus on first-generation immigrants . . . Many business writings are framed as cutthroat; impressively, the opposite is true here, as the book focuses instead on the inspirational, often emphasizing aiding others who seek to become entrepreneurs and giving back to the community.

— Kirkus Review

John Shen's book is not only a remarkable personal journey leading to understanding, wisdom, and ultimately enlightenment to become an outstanding entrepreneur and innovator, but it is much more. John's strength is his intuitive understanding of empathy.

— Ira Kurzban, Attorney At Law

This book encompasses a multitude of valuable lessons in the realm of business . . . both a source of motivation and entrepreneurial awareness by presenting the life of a successful innovator and his journey to success . . . highly recommend this book to new startups in the business world (who) can benefit from adopting the author's leadership culture.

— Online Bookclub Review

I highly recommend *Crossing the Swamp* for any startup founder who seeks inspiration and valuable insights into entrepreneurial success. John Shen provides clear, actionable advice that proves he knows the inner life of an entrepreneur.

—Simon Pang, Co-founder, Royal Business Bank,
1st generation immigrant entrepreneur

CROSSING THE SWAMP

Crossing the Swamp

MY PATH TO INNOVATING AS A
PARALLEL ENTREPRENEUR

JOHN SHEN

Precocity Press

Editorial Direction and Editing: Rick Benzel
Copyediting: Julie Simpson, OnWords & UpWords!
Creative Direction: Susan Shankin
Cover and Book Design: Susan Shankin and Elizabeth Lenthall
Typesetting: Andrea Reider
Illustrations: Tim Kummerow
Chart: Richard Sheppard

Published by Precocity Press, Los Angeles, CA

Printed in Hong Kong SAR

ISBN: 979-8-9877766-7-4 (Hardcover)
ISBN: 979-8-9877766-1-2 (Paperback)
ISBN: 979-8-9877766-2-9 (eBook)

Library of Congress Control Number: 2023904673

Contents

To entrepreneurs who struggle to build businesses
and those who simply have a big dream
but face challenges in their lives . . .

CROSSING THE SWAMP

Overview of My Story

John Shen

It had been one of the worst days of my life. I had come to Hawaii in a last-gasp effort to sell land I owned in Florida, where I had been in the real estate business. The economic crisis of 2007–2008 had devastated the highly successful real estate agency and mortgage broker business I had founded and had been operating for the past five years in the Orlando area. I was in dire straits, unable to sell a single house or close a mortgage deal.

Despite the real estate market crash on the mainland, Hawaiians had always been eager to buy land in Florida — or so I thought. I had been out all morning trying to persuade potential investors, but no one was attracted to the land deals I offered. I had dialed through the contact list on my cell phone and sent scores of emails, but every reply was negative. It was bad news after bad news.

I realized I would have to close my Orlando offices within a month. My bank accounts were nearly empty. I had huge credit card debt. Most of all, the reputation I had worked hard to develop as a respected and talented successful entrepreneur in Orlando was evaporating in front of my eyes. It would be the end of the world for me. How could I possibly create my business success again?

As I gazed out the window of my hotel in Honolulu, I thought about the journey I had made from my childhood in Beijing to this day in 2008. From my perch on the 16th floor, I faced the vast expanse of the Pacific Ocean, aware that I could easily fly over the horizon if I chose to return to the life I had decades ago with my family in China. Below me, mainland tourists, unaware of what was about to happen above them, made their way across the city's streets dotted with shops and tall royal palms. It was a calm Hawaiian afternoon, not the kind of day for someone to jump 16 floors to their death.

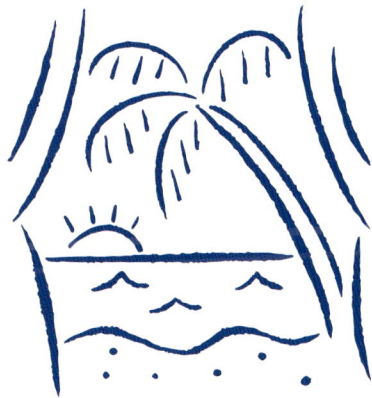

When people are thinking of committing suicide, their head is not clear. The human self-preservation instinct normally keeps us from doing crazy things. But when you become so despondent that life does not seem to matter anymore, that instinct is overpowered. You cannot face reality. You want to leave everything behind.

I opened the window and put my foot on the sill, contemplating the only choice I believed I had. It was time to put a stop to my embarrassment and pain. I was ready to die and end my enormous failure.

■ ■ ■ ■ ■

Why miracles happen to some but not others, I cannot explain. I was one of the fortunate. I had been mired in the proverbial swamp of failure when a lifeline was thrown my way.

As I was readying my body to jump, I knocked against my laptop on the table next to the window. The screen flashed on and the junk folder of my email account was visible. I was inexplicably drawn to look at a spam email whose subject line was something like "Need Inspiration? Read 'A Glass of Water.'" Perhaps inwardly, I still wanted to cling to life, or maybe my brain was so crazy I wanted my last act on earth to be spent reading spam emails. I was curious what the email had to say.

Why miracles happen to some but not others, I cannot explain. I was one of the fortunate.

I got off the sill, stepped away from the window, and read the item. It told the story of a coach teaching a class about how people can deal with pressure. As he walked into the classroom, a glass of water was waiting for the coach at the lectern. He asked the audience to guess how much the water weighed. The students shouted out answers: 8 ounces, 12 ounces, and so on. He told them that the actual net weight does not matter; what counts is how long you have to hold the glass. If you hold it for just one second, it is not heavy. But if you must hold it for 24 hours, your arm will go numb.

The story went on to make the following analogy. The pressures we feel during our life are like the glass of water. Their net weight is not what matters; it's how long we hold on to those pressures. If we hold them for a long time, and even add more pressure each day, the total weight will be forever increasing. We may think we enjoy carrying this pressure, and so we don't get rid of it, but we will eventually crack under its weight.

The coach explained to the students that we each face different pressures every day. But we do not need to keep carrying their weight. We can choose to put it down literally *in a single second* if we want to.

When I read that sentence, something clicked in my mind and reversed my attitude. I no longer wished to end my life. I realized that I could alter my perception about my problems. I could release the pressure I was facing in a single second if I put my mind to it.

I closed the window and sat down and cried; then I picked up my cell phone and called a friend of mine who lived in Honolulu. Earlier that week, he had invited me to a send-off party in honor of his son who had been accepted at Purdue University and was getting ready to leave for school. I had originally turned down his invitation because I was so busy and my mind was full of my business troubles. But after reading the Glass of Water story, I knew I had no choice but to leave all my problems behind so I could survive. I told my friend I would attend and he was thrilled. At that particular moment, I was so grateful for catching that email. The party that night turned out to be everything I needed to start a new chapter of my life.

I have lost my friend's contact information since then; we no longer stay in touch. He may never find out exactly what he did for me that night but going to that party was how I put the water down. It was my sanctuary, a safe place where I could release all the pressure I was holding inside. I found immense joy in being around the youthful energy of my friend's son and his friends, all of them excited about graduating high school and going to college. I was no longer feeling despondent about my life; the party infused in me an amazing sense of hope. No one could have possibly guessed that just hours before, I had been ready to jump out the window of a high-rise hotel.

■ ■ ■ ■ ■

My near suicide occurred in 2008 and it is now 2023. Obviously I am still here on earth, grateful that I did not take my own life. I have since rebuilt myself and my businesses far beyond what I lost in the real estate market crash of 2007 — and far beyond what I ever imagined for myself.

John Shen

Since 2008, I have travelled

an amazing journey to

entrepreneurial success.

I am not just an entrepreneur,

but a "parallel entrepreneur."

I have founded five companies

and have garnered numerous

accolades from major media.

Since 2008, I have travelled an amazing journey to entrepreneurial success. I am not just an entrepreneur, but a "parallel entrepreneur." I have founded five companies and have garnered numerous accolades from major media; my businesses have been highlighted among the Fastest Growing Companies and The Best Places to Work every year in prestigious publications such as the *Financial Times* and *INC.* magazine. I am widely recognized by various professional networks and respected in the southern California community as a financial engineer, a visionary, and a leader in foreign direct investments, small business lending, innovation and entrepreneurship, trust business operation, and virtual/ghost kitchen development, among other fields. By the end of 2022, my businesses, collectively, have provided small business loans to over 30,000 small businesses across all 50 states, created or retained over 120,000 jobs nationwide, and invested or helped hundreds of early-stage startups. In 2022, as an accomplished Asian-American community leader, I had a chance to meet President Biden and was then invited to the White House four times within the year to attend various events: a critical legislation signing, the July 4th celebration, the annual congressional picnic, and the 2022 Christmas party.

Accolades and Awards

- Awarded 2023 California Financial Services Executive of the Year and Man of the Year in the field of finance, both by *Top 100 Registry*.

- Sunstone Management and American Lending Center ranked on the *Financial Times* report, The Americas' Fastest Growing Companies, beating out the likes of Facebook, Tesla, Uber, Airbnb, and other tech giants in terms of revenue growth rate in 2023, 2022, and 2021.

- ACL made the *INC 5000* list of fastest-growing private companies in America, as ranked by revenue growth, in 2020–2023, while Sunstone made this list in 2020–2022.

- 2023 and 2022 C-suite Visionary by the *Los Angeles Times*.

- Awarded 2022 Distinguished Leader in Wealth Management by *Orange County Business Journal*.

- In June 2022, I had the honor of being invited to meet with President Biden, and hosted Vice-President Harris at my home representing the Asian American Pacific Islanders (AAPI) community.

- Among the 2021 recipients of the Albert Nelson Marquis Lifetime Achievement Award in Marquis *Who's Who*.

- In 2017, I was awarded the SBA 504 Lender of the Year accolade by the Coleman Report, a national award in the banking industry.

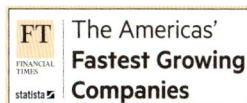

My Journey to Success

Many people wanting to be entrepreneurs have approached me and asked how I came to achieve my success. Some know that I am an immigrant to America, arriving here just three decades ago. People are surprised that I own and operate so many companies at once and want to understand how it can possibly be. What kind of superpowers do I have, they wonder.

I am not special. I have no actual superpowers. But I do have insights and advice to offer anyone who dreams of becoming an entrepreneur or is in the midst of launching a startup venture. I'm writing this book to share my entrepreneurial journey because I believe anyone can do what I have done. In the course of my career spanning nearly 30 years, I have learned the lessons of how to start and grow profitable companies—and how to come back from failure. I am opening up my life story to everyone, and by doing so I hope to inspire you so you can do the same.

The story of my near suicide after the collapse of my real estate business is the first foundational lesson I want to impart:

Never give in to desperation.

If you experience a business downturn or an outright failure, you do not need to keep holding on to the pressure. Learn, as I did, to let go of the weight you are holding *in a single second* so you can focus on solving the problems in front of you. For me, knowing how to release stress and pressure has become one of the key strengths that allows me to remain calm while running multiple companies. In a much broader sense, the "Glass of Water" story taught me an invaluable life philosophy. After practicing it so many times, I have become a master of removing pressure instantly and everywhere in my life. This helps me stay positive while handling my work; but more importantly, it takes away any negativity from my personal life as well, filling it with complete joy and happiness.

I have learned that overcoming difficulties is like crossing a swamp. At first, the mud is thick and the water is deep, and every step is a struggle. But with persistence, each step gets a little easier, and eventually, you start to see the other side. You may have to veer off course, navigate around obstacles, and sometimes even take a step backward, but as long as you keep moving forward, you'll eventually reach dry land. And when you finally emerge from the other side of the swamp, you'll be stronger, more resilient, and ready to take on whatever challenges come your way.

My goal in sharing my life story and my advice is to support the growing interest in entrepreneurship in the US. In my view, those who start new businesses are the lifeblood of this country. For roughly the past two decades, the ranks of entrepreneurs have skyrocketed, not just in the US, but around the world. The COVID-19 pandemic further increased the desire among millions of people to leave their jobs and start their own businesses. The need to solve thousands of problems in the world requires innovation—and that is the work of the rising number of entrepreneurs, whom I seek to support.

Entrepreneur Statistics

Here's inspiration for you. Consider these interesting statistics about entrepreneurship worldwide.

- It is estimated that in 2022, 33 million Americans were starting or already running their own businesses, up from 25 million in 2016. This comes out to about 16% of the US workforce.

- In 2021, more than 5.4 million new businesses were registered, up from 4.3 million in 2020, an increase of 23%.

- The entrepreneurship failure has never been lower; only 20% of new businesses close after one year, though 50% fail within five years.

- There are an estimated 582 million entrepreneurs in the world.

- Entrepreneurs in the US tend to be between the ages of 25 and 44, motivated by their desire to pursue a passion, exit a corporate job, and capitalize on new opportunities.

- 70% of entrepreneurs have gone to college, but 30% have not.

- 55% of adults in the US have started at least one business in their lifetime.

- 26% of adults in the US have started two or more businesses in their lifetime.

- The average entrepreneur in the US starts their first business when they are 42, but that age varies by industry. In the software industry, the average age is 40. In the oil and gas industry, it's closer to 47.

- It's never too late to start a business:
  - 13% of Americans between the ages of 45 and 54 started new businesses in 2019.
  - Similarly, 13% of Americans between the ages of 55 and 64 started new businesses in 2019.
  - 6% of Americans between the ages of 65 and 74 started new businesses in 2019.

My Growing Interest in Supporting Entrepreneurs and Startups

My work today as the leader of multiple companies brings me immense joy and pleasure. It's fun! My life as the CEO of American Lending Center (ALC), and chairman of the board of all my companies, is challenging, stimulating, and exciting. My executive teams and I work very hard to scope out new opportunities for our companies, each of us bringing new ideas and amazing energies to our work. We share a collective commitment to service, community, and innovation.

In particular, I've developed a strong passion for helping new entrepreneurs develop and grow their businesses in the earliest stages. Since 2018, I have been building unique partnerships with local governments and academic institutions that teach innovation and entrepreneurship. With the desired end result being to mentor entrepreneurs and link them up with investors, these partnerships focus on encouraging startup communities in various ways: through student and faculty pitch competitions, demo days, and, most importantly, competitive tech accelerator programs. (See sidebar on page 16.)

In 2019, my company Sunstone Management started a multi-year sponsorship with California State University Long Beach (CSULB) for its historic "pitch competition" program, now called the Sunstone Innovation Challenge. That sponsorship paved the way for two unprecedented annual programs launched in 2022: Sunstone CSU Startup Launch and CSU Demo Day. Sunstone Management was the named sponsor for both events, which showcase early-stage startups emerging in the California State University system across all 23 of its campuses. These events are now on track to become the most impactful innovation and entrepreneurial activities in the higher education system in California.

In 2021, as an alumna of the Paul Merage School of Business at the University of California Irvine (UCI), my wife and COO of ALC, Stella Zhang, made a donation to her alma mater to sponsor the New Venture Competition, the most attended student pitch competition in Orange County. The event was renamed the Stella Zhang New Venture Competition. In the 2021-22 season alone, this event attracted the participation of approximately 100 student teams on the UCI campus and made a lasting impact on the future career development of these young entrepreneurs.

As Sunstone Management and my family continue to expand our sponsorship and support for many other on-campus pitch competitions, we also have rapidly developed new opportunities to sponsor a few highly influential demo day events across California. In 2021, my company Partake Collective sponsored the first demo day event in the history of the University of California system, Born in California, hosted by UCI Beall Applied Innovation. Starting in 2022, Sunstone Management took over the sponsorship and became the main driving force of this incredible marketplace, which was created to provide direct capital access to early-stage startups thriving in the University of California system covering 10 of the most renowned research universities in the world.

I have long believed that a tech accelerator is the most efficient program to foster the growth of early-stage startups. It also serves as an effective investment tool for investors to target and select disruptive companies that have the best potential to experience explosive valuation growth in the future. The investment success of the first-generation accelerators such as Y-Combinator (started in 2005) and Tech Stars (started in 2006) motivated me to look into this young but fast-evolving industry. My own research showed an incredible demand for accelerator operations across the country and all over the world. In 2019, I decided to build new accelerators. But how?

The scope and quality of the services of an accelerator largely depend on the access and management of local entrepreneurial resources. For instance, an accelerator must recruit high-quality, oftentimes sector-specific experts to serve as mentors of the cohort members. It is a short-term (normally 3–6 months) training program but there is much that needs to be built into the program so that the cohort members can quickly learn and accelerate in the most critical stage of the businesses. The resources my companies can bring in are simply not enough. My strategies? I turned to the local governments and university partners.

In early 2018, I sat down with John Keisler, who then was the director of economic development for the City of Long Beach, and Wade Martin, director of the Institute for Innovation and Entrepreneurship at California State University Long Beach. That conversation eventually created the first accelerator program in the US (and possibly the world) based on a unique "public-private-education" (PPE) partnership. It leverages the power of all three parties to provide strong community support and incredible operational resources to the Long Beach Accelerator.™ The Long Beach Accelerator has already achieved more success than anyone could have possibly expected when it opened in 2019, thanks to its unique PPE model.

In 2022, Sunstone Management was able to build five other accelerators using the exact same formula. All of these accelerators are growing fast and are financially healthy. Collectively, this innovative concept has made immediate contributions to the American startup community in a number of positive ways.

I moved my offices from Long Beach to Irvine, California in October 2021 and I have committed to the Irvine and Orange County community that our multiple companies will help support one of the fastest growing and most dynamic innovation and entrepreneurial ecosystems anywhere in the USA.

From my office in the Airport Tower in Irvine, I can no longer imagine why I would ever have considered ending my life after just one failure. When you want to be an entrepreneur, failure is actually halfway to success. You just have to keep marching and learn to release the stress and pressure on you in one second.

Startup Terms

1. *Pitch Competition.* An event that has a number of presentations of startup business plans, often including innovative concepts to develop new products or services in emerging markets, usually hosted by an academic institution. Students and young entrepreneurs, alone or in teams, participate to win prizes and gain support and resources to launch their new businesses.

2. *Demo Day.* An event where early-stage startups already in business present their companies in pursuit of equity and other types of investment from investors and venture capitalists.

3. *Tech Accelerator.* A short-term competitive training program that provides comprehensive resources to help startups accelerate their growth in their early stages. Assistance includes financial support, mentoring, classes on entrepreneurship, and networking.

Three Unique Perspectives

One can read dozens of books about how to succeed as an entrepreneur, so why should you read this one? My answer is that I believe what I have to share is unique and differs significantly from what other books or courses will offer you, in three ways.

DIFFERENCE 1:
LIFE EXPERIENCE AS AN ENTREPRENEUR

First and foremost, the insights and advice I offer are based on my real-life experience as an entrepreneur. I did not go to business school to earn an MBA, so my business knowledge and leadership skills have been acquired from decades of hard work starting companies and growing their revenues and profitability. I did earn a master's degree in statistics and decision sciences from Duke University, but I do not attribute my entrepreneurial success to having this degree. My achievements today derive not from classroom smarts but from actually being on the front lines of startup businesses, where I have, out of necessity, done everything myself. I have waded in the swamp of failure and crossed it to achieve my entrepreneurial dreams.

COMPANY A

Start ⟶ Exit

COMPANY B

Start ⟶ Exit

COMPANY C

Start ⟶ Exit

DIFFERENCE 2: BECOMING A PARALLEL ENTREPRENEUR

This book provides advice on the newest trend in entrepreneurship: becoming not just a solo entrepreneur, or a serial entrepreneur, but a *parallel entrepreneur*. What are the distinctions between these?

When most people think about being an entrepreneur, the usual perception is that it is about being a "solo entrepreneur." This is the image of someone who launches one startup venture and transforms it into a great success that is then sold for a large profit, creating enormous wealth for the founder and perhaps leading to an early retirement and a life of leisure.

PARALLEL ENTREPRENEUR

COMPANY A

Start ⟶ Growing ⟶ Growing ⟶ Exit
                                    (but not necessarily)

John Shen

But today we also hear about those who seem to be dissatisfied with starting just one company. They become "serial entrepreneurs," i.e., someone with a creative idea who launches a startup that he or she transforms into a successful business. The serial entrepreneur then sells that business, and shortly thereafter launches another startup, which also becomes successful. Some serial entrepreneurs may hold on to their first business for some time, to increase its value before selling it while also launching their second business. The most creative, innovative, and prolific serial entrepreneurs may launch three, four, even five or more businesses over their lifetime, selling each one for substantial profits. Each cash infusion becomes part of the capital they need to launch the next business. The feat of starting one business after another is what makes them serial entrepreneurs. They thrive on launching company after company, enriching themselves magnificently along the way. These entrepreneurs are bold and innovative, and I applaud their successes.

But the unique element that I focus on in this book is my experience of being a *parallel entrepreneur*. This term refers to an entrepreneur who seeks to launch and *simultaneously* operate many companies, with no intention of "flipping them" as soon as they become profitable. To my knowledge, being a parallel entrepreneur is a rather new concept. Most people do not understand the term when I use it to describe the role that I have as CEO of one company and chairman of the board of several others.

COMPANY B

Start ⟶ Growing ⟶ Growing

COMPANY C

Start ⟶ Growing

The goal of the parallel entrepreneur is to take advantage of the potential synergies, of which there are many, among all their businesses. The parallel entrepreneur thrives on the excitement of running many businesses all at the same time, going from one to another. Their job is more like playing chess, where you need to pay attention to the interactions of many pieces at once, rather than, say, a card game where one card is thrown at a time.

The goal of the parallel entrepreneur is to take advantage of potential synergies, of which there are many, among all their businesses.

I believe parallel entrepreneurship will become the most popular trend among young entrepreneurs. In my view, once you start one company and bring it to a certain level of success, you are ideally positioned to leverage your knowledge, your staff, your customers, or your market dominance to start yet another company. Frankly, if you have the intelligence and stamina to be a solo entrepreneur, you might as well aim to be a parallel one. The benefits of "going parallel" are enormous, as I will explain in the coming chapters. As you will also see, it is not as difficult to achieve multiple successes—and it is truly more exciting, challenging, and intellectually stimulating.

DIFFERENCE 3: FIRST-GENERATION IMMIGRANT FOCUS

The third unique element of this book arises from the fact that I am a first-generation immigrant entrepreneur in America. I was born and grew up in Beijing and spent my youth knowing almost nothing about America. I spoke only broken English when I arrived in the US to attend the Duke University PhD program in sociology, which after the first year I changed to the master's program in statistics. I never imagined that I would start a business, much less many of them, when I completed my MS degree at Duke.

When you are an immigrant in America, nothing comes easy. Depending on where you are from, you face a range of cultural differences, some of which are trivial, but many of which are enormously difficult to surmount. If you are from Europe, it may be easier to fit into the American culture because your Western values are fairly similar. But if you are from Asia or Africa, your native culture is worlds apart from how Americans think and act. Your challenges are compounded by differences in thinking style, values, attitudes, and language barriers.

Being born in China, I was raised not to question authorities such as parents, teachers, professors, government officials, or actually anyone. The average Chinese person is respectful, unassuming, and unaggressive, qualities that do not always serve you well when you start your own business. I was not from a wealthy family, so I did not have an upbringing where money dripped off my nose or imbued me with gentlemanly habits, social graces, or a commanding presence. I landed in America as a shy, introverted Chinese student who got lucky enough to win a full scholarship to one of the top American universities. If I didn't succeed here, I would have had to go back to China; I would have been forced to leave the US once my student visa expired.

In writing this book, I thus also want to highlight the special challenges that first-generation immigrants must face when starting an entrepreneurial venture in the US. By "first generation," I am referring to immigrants who, like me, may have arrived in the US as students and then stayed to start a job or become an entrepreneur. According to one statistic, in 2020, six out of every 1,000 immigrants to the US started a new business!

I also include immigrants who were brought here as children by their parents who arrived in America (legally or illegally). I would also add here children of first-generation immigrants. Although, technically speaking, they are second-generation immigrants, since their parents were new to America and often did not learn English, these children must make it on their own, just like first-generation immigrants.

Based on my experience as a first-generation immigrant, I am convinced that the journey to success is more challenging, more taxing on the mind and body, and often more frustrating when you are essentially a foreigner. It took me years to begin to feel, think, and act like other Americans, but I am as proud to be an American as any other person in this country.

As immigrants, you may often wonder if it is easier and less painful psychologically to just return to your native country and start a business there. I frequently asked myself that. You may be frustrated that people do not seem to understand your broken English or follow your thought process. You may feel embarrassed or even angry if others do not listen to you or pay attention to your ideas because they view you as a foreigner who doesn't deserve to be in America. You may encounter moments of prejudice because of your ethnicity or race. The worst is, you may experience severe depression if your business fails and you feel that you have disappointed family members back home who helped you come to the US or invested in your business.

Based on my experience as
a first-generation immigrant,
I am convinced
that the journey to success
is more challenging,
more taxing on the mind
and body, and often
more frustrating when
you are essentially
a foreigner.

Let me clarify my opinion. In no uncertain terms, it is all worth it if you are a first-generation immigrant. America is the greatest country in the world to be an entrepreneur. The opportunities to create businesses are among the best; the potential for building a good life with wealth is available to anyone who desires it; and the rewards of freedom for you and your family are unbeatable.

FIRST-GENERATION SUCCESSFUL IMMIGRANT ENTREPRENEURS

In 2022, the Massachusetts Institute of Technology released a study indicating that immigrants are 80% more likely to found a company, compared to natural-born Americans. According to other research, about 25% of all entrepreneurs in the US are immigrants. And the National Foundation for American Policy, a nonprofit research institute that tracks trade and immigration, states that immigrants have started 319 of 582 (55%) of America's privately held startups whose values are over $1 billion. The Fortune 500 list includes 216 companies founded by immigrants. Here's a partial list of companies whose founders are either first-generation immigrants or children of first-generation immigrants.

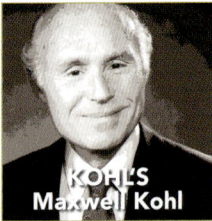

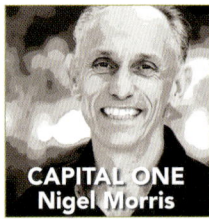

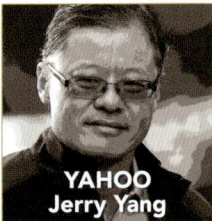

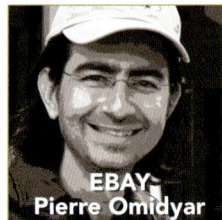

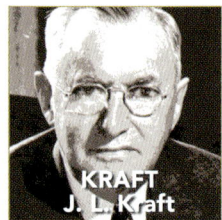

KOHL'S
Maxwell Kohl

CAPITAL ONE
Nigel Morris

YAHOO
Jerry Yang

STAX
Suneera Madhani

APPLE
Steve Jobs

QUALCOMM
Irwin M. Jacobs

EBAY
Pierre Omidyar

GOOGLE
Sergey Brin

AMAZON
Jeff Bezos

KRAFT
J. L. Kraft

What Is an Entrepreneur?

The term "entrepreneur" has its origins in the Latin verb *prehendere*, which means "to seize" or "take control." The word was actually used to describe the military strategy of surrounding a town to conquer it.

Using the word as we do today—to signify someone who creates a new business, taking on risks in exchange for potential large rewards—first occurred in 1803 in a treatise by a French economist, Jean-Baptiste Say. He acknowledged how those who own small businesses make significant contributions to their nation's economy.

But we all know that the term implies much more than that. An entrepreneur may invent or create the idea that becomes the basis for the business, or the idea can derive from trends that the entrepreneur recognizes and seizes upon to form the business. Finally, an entrepreneur is usually the person who not only starts the business but also leads it as the chief executive officer, leader, founding partner, or general manager, whichever title fits best.

The father of modern entrepreneurship, however, is the twentieth-century economist Joseph Schumpeter, who is considered the first to recognize how entrepreneurs *disrupt* the business world by introducing innovations that replace existing technologies and processes. This idea of disruption is a key concept in entrepreneurship today. Schumpeter's term "creative destruction" has come to symbolize how a constant stream of new technologies from upstart startups can easily take down the biggest companies of the world that once controlled a market. A well-known example of this is the collapse of Blockbuster Video, replaced by upstart Netflix. In recent times, the rise of e-commerce has disrupted the retail industry in nearly every field. Smartphones have replaced desktops and laptops. Augmented Reality and Virtual Reality (AR/VR) are expected to become the next disruptive technologies.

The Eight Talents for Success in Entrepreneurship

No one would deny that entrepreneurship requires hard work. In fact, in the beginning, it's pretty much nothing but hard work and long hours for months and years on end. Most people prefer to have a job and a salary compared to taking on the risks and burdens of starting their own business. Taking the leap from having a job to starting your own venture can be anxiety-provoking.

But creating a successful company (or more than one) is not like doing time in prison; just putting in the time is not enough. There are specific personal qualities, or "talents" as I call them, that are necessary to build the personal foundation and structure for success.

Many business articles and books have sought to identify these qualities; they typically will say they include, for example, being innovative, being creative, possessing quick decision-making skills, having leadership traits, and exhibiting "intuitive" capabilities to take the right actions.

From my experience, I would not include some of those talents on a list of traits necessary for entrepreneurial success. For instance, I believe that entrepreneurs should not make quick decisions; they need to be thoughtful and take the necessary time to evaluate long-term results, not short-term gains. Entrepreneurs also do not need to have native leadership skills, as they can develop them with experience, as I did.

The chapters of this book identify what I consider the eight top talents critical for entrepreneurial success. My experience is that you do not need to be born with these qualities. I was certainly not born with all of them. I did not have them all as a child in China, nor did I have all these talents when I started my first business in 2002. But just as I did,

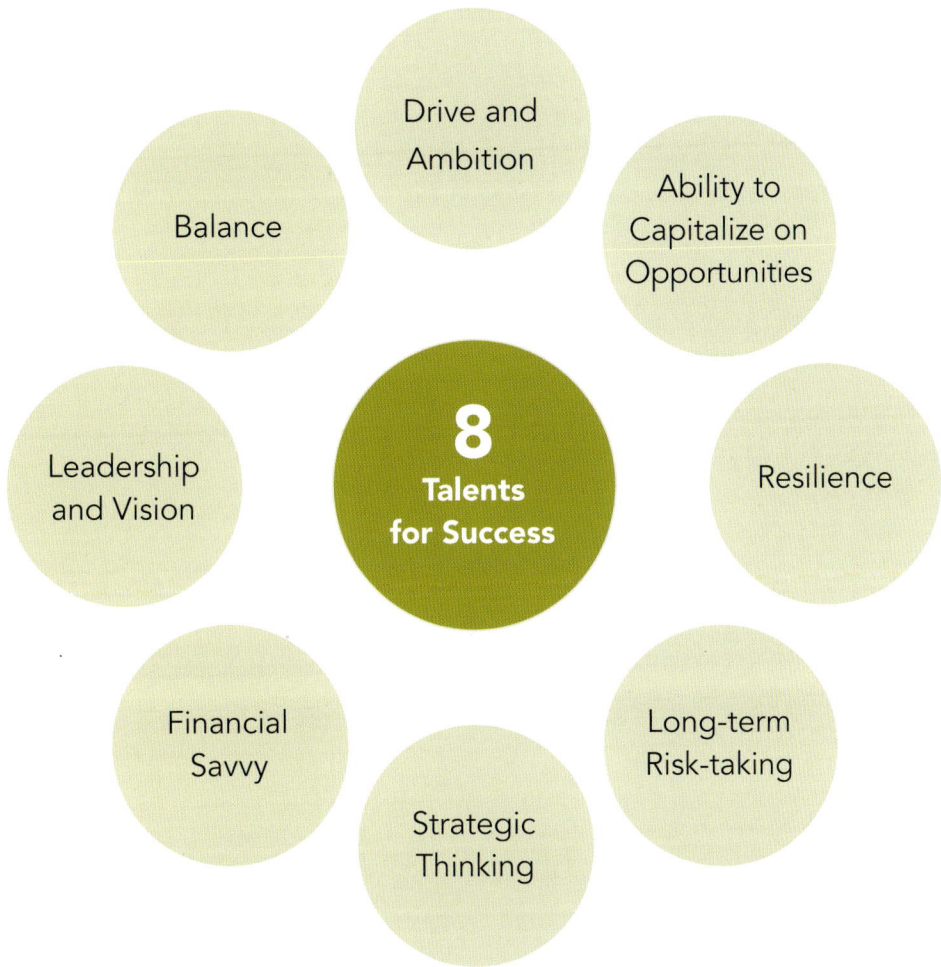

8
Talents
for Success

Drive and Ambition

Ability to Capitalize on Opportunities

Resilience

Long-term Risk-taking

Strategic Thinking

Financial Savvy

Leadership and Vision

Balance

you can seek to develop and improve these eight talents over time, strengthening them day by day along your journey from launching a solo startup to becoming a successful parallel entrepreneur.

As you read about these talents, you will also learn the very personal story about how I arrived at my current point in life. Each of the chapters tells an episode of my journey to entrepreneurial success, with total honesty about the various challenges and failures along the way. I share my personal story with the hope that it can inspire all readers, especially those like me who are first-generation immigrants in the US with high hopes of living the American Dream.

Here is an overview of the chapters:

Drive and Ambition

Chapter 1. Drive is the internal force that pushes you forward to change your life and determine your own future. Entrepreneurs must feel ambitious and driven inside to overcome whatever challenges are thrown at them and to come out on top in the end. You will read the story of my childhood and youth in China and why I became driven to leave my native country to come to the US to study and change my life.

Ability to Capitalize on Opportunities

Chapter 2. This is a talent that derives from being watchful and perceptive about events in the world that could represent opportunities for your current company, a future business on your road to becoming an entrepreneur, or additional companies you can build as you move towards being a parallel entrepreneur.

Resilience

Chapter 3. Resilience is a key talent for the entrepreneurial personality. Failure is endemic in entrepreneurship, so you must have the inner calm and fortitude required to be able to overcome setbacks of any kind, even those that include losing your entire business. Resilience is the quality that enables you to cross the swamp.

Long-term Risk-taking

Chapter 4. Risk-taking is endemic to entrepreneurship, but I have learned that the smartest way to think about taking risks must be based on long-term results. Chasing short-term payoffs may appear to be attractive, but my experience shows that the risk of failure behind any short-term opportunity could be far higher than you imagine, and certainly much higher than a long-term one of the same nature. In fact, most business operations consist of a number of projects that serve different purposes. What most people do not seem to understand is that the risk of failure behind long-term projects is usually minimal. If you can minimize the risk on each of the projects you undertake, you will have a significantly higher chance to win big in the end. The best strategy is therefore to always work on projects to pursue long-term goals. If you keep doing this, you are almost certain to ultimately succeed.

Strategic Thinking

Chapter 5. While having the ability to capitalize on opportunities requires strategic thinking, I am referring in this chapter to two additional types of strategic thinking that I believe are necessary for entrepreneurs. The first relates to learning how to *leverage*. The second focuses on the ability to *innovate*, coming up with new ideas to improve your own business systems, processes, and methods of achieving your goals. In fact, leveraging and innovating go hand in hand, as you will learn in this chapter. I will also profile several of the CEOs who lead my companies, including John Keisler, CEO of Sunstone Management; and Adam Carrillo, CEO of Partake Collective. You will see how each of these executives has worked with me to leverage and innovate.

Financial Savvy

Chapter 6. There is a paradoxical financial truth about entrepreneurship that I will share in this chapter. Your financial success should not be judged by your company's profits, but rather by its revenues. I will explain why focusing on increasing your revenues provides faster short-term results and better long-term growth. I will also discuss several other elements of what I consider to be financial savvy: selecting the right office space to attract the best employees and serve the right customers; deciding whether to self-fund your business or seek external investors; learning how to turn crisis into opportunity; and structuring your business for optimum income potential while minimizing the tax implications.

Leadership and Vision

Chapter 7. Most people are not born leaders, yet being an entrepreneur requires you to develop this talent. In this chapter, I share five Leadership Advice lessons that I believe are pivotal to successfully managing any young company. One of these focuses on how to be a visionary, by which I mean someone who can recognize far in advance, and before others, potential new trends that could become the next profitable business opportunity. You will also learn why being a parallel entrepreneur actually improves your visionary skills because you can peruse a wider horizon of trends when you operate multiple companies.

Balance

Chapter 8. Chasing success in business takes a toll on your soul. This chapter is about the most personal matters of your life: your marriage or relationship, your family, your mental and physical health, managing your time, and never forgetting what counts most in life. I discuss how to balance work and home life when you work with your spouse, and you will read an interview with my wife, Stella Zhang, COO of ALC.

Whether you are just starting out or are years into creating your venture, my goal is to help you integrate these eight talents into your life, recalling them whenever you need inspiration or practical guidance to overcome a problem or advance your business into its next phase of growth. I am confident anyone can learn and master them, as each plays a key role in developing a successful, sustainable business.

I wish every reader of this book good fortune. May your dreams to start a business, innovate something new, create wealth and jobs for yourself and others, and improve the quality of life in your community or in the world come true. Finally, never let setbacks or failure deter you from achieving success. You can cross the swamp, just as I did.

CHAPTER 1

Drive and Ambition

DRIVE

- To propel or carry along by force in a specified direction

- An innate, biologically determined urge to attain a goal
  or satisfy a need

- Synonym: ambition

John Shen

It is often said that entrepreneurs need to have *passion*. I suggest it is more than that—they must be *driven!*

There is a distinction between the two. You can have a passion for computers, finance, architecture, rockets, or books. But passion alone does not create successful entrepreneurs. Passion does not turn you into the CEO of a software company, a bank, a construction and engineering company, a jet engine developer, or an international publishing company. What makes reaching that kind of successful leadership position possible in any industry is an unstoppable drive to do the hard work needed to achieve your goal.

Being driven means you do not accept where you are right now. Wherever you are, there is a something better out there, a new destination to reach. And then when you get there, you see that there is yet another new destination.

Being driven can derive from a force inside you that does not let you stop changing something you can improve. Or it might be an internal voice telling you to build something that does not exist. Being driven as an entrepreneur means wanting to go beyond having a job, or just working for yourself in a little retail shop you own. It's a craving to start a "real" company with some (or a lot of) employees, creating a well-known brand, building a respected reputation, and leaving a lasting mark during your time on earth.

The end result of entrepreneurial drive is progress. Without the entrepreneurs of the past, we would still be living in the pre-industrial age. Entrepreneurs create new technologies, new processes, and new systems that build on or improve how things were done before. Entrepreneurs contribute to the economy by creating jobs, salaries,

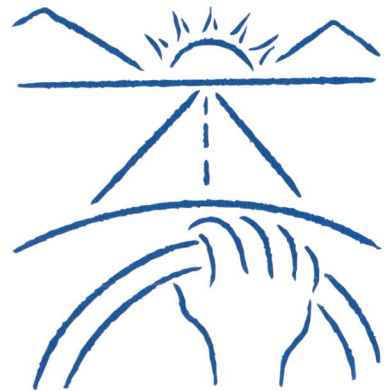

benefits, and tax income. Concerned socially conscious entrepreneurs today increasingly seek to solve a societal problem or improve the environment.

If you want to be an entrepreneur, you cannot just be a tire-kicker. You have to buy the car and drive it.

If you want to be a full-fledged entrepreneur, you need a strong infusion of drive to overcome the inertia of life. Just having passion doesn't cut it. Every day, creative people develop ideas and innovations that could result in a startup business, but they don't follow through. They remind me of people who want to buy a new car and go to the dealership to look. They walk around the models on display and kick the tires, but in the end they turn away from buying. Many would-be entrepreneurs are "tire-kickers." When they get an idea, they walk around it . . . and then walk away.

John Shen

It is often thought entrepreneurs are born with natural drive; this makes them different, more talented than other people. I disagree. I believe anyone can develop the strong degree of drive it takes to be an entrepreneur. Your drive may not be there at birth, but all it takes is a spark to light it. Like a cold engine that ignites from a spark plug, there often comes an event or a person in someone's life that suddenly inspires that individual to find the drive of an entrepreneurial go-getter.

I have seen this talent come alive in the hundreds of people who have participated in the startup pitch competitions, demo days, and tech accelerators that my company has been involved with, either as a sponsor or a capital partner. These young entrepreneurs are competitive, goal-driven, and eager to transform their innovative idea into a real company.

If you want to be a full-fledged entrepreneur, you need a strong infusion of drive to overcome the inertia of life. Just having passion doesn't cut it.

I also know the deep need for drive from my own personal experience of going from working at a salaried job to realizing that I wanted to start a business. Your drive to start a business venture has to be more forceful in your mind than any other option available to you. To understand the origins of my drive, I share my personal life story in hopes that it can inspire you, whatever your background.

My Drive for a Better Life

I was not born with the drive to be an entrepreneur, as this was impossible in 1970, the year of my birth. Chairman Mao Zedong ruled China for decades (1949–1976) with an iron fist. During the final years of his extreme totalitarian dictatorship, the Great Proletarian Cultural Revolution, the movement launched by Mao in 1966, sought to purge any form of capitalism from China. No such thing as an entrepreneur could exist in Mao's society.

I was fortunate that my parents were hard-working, obedient people who followed the rules and did not risk being sent to "retraining camps," which Mao created for those whom he sought to punish. My father was a highly respected professor of Chinese literature at Peking University and my mother a high school teacher. You might think that having intellectual, professional parents made us a middle-class family, but not in Mao's China. My parents' combined salary was about $20 per month. We lived with my older brother in a two-room apartment in a four-story building housing about 47 other families. Ours was far from a privileged life, but I had a happy childhood and at least we had food and clothing, unlike many Chinese families in that period of time, when millions of Chinese starved to death or lived in abject poverty.

To attend my elementary school, I had to walk for one hour four times a day, since we came home for lunch and had to return to school and remain there until 5:00 pm. When I got to junior high, I was allowed to ride my bike to school, which saved a lot of time.

I was not among the smartest students for most of my early years of education. I was a daydreamer in class and after school preferred playing with friends. I was shy and was often bullied by bigger kids. My life's dream at this time was to be just like my parents, having a steady job so I could watch TV at night and cook my own dinners. That was my idea of success. I never imagined being a successful and wealthy entrepreneur by American standards.

However, somewhere around 12 years old, *the drive to excel* clicked in me. It was an unexpected spark that ignited my ambition. I suddenly became very serious and studious. I knew my parents worked hard all day. In the evenings after dinner, I watched them grading papers and preparing their classes. In Beijing, you had to take an exam to get into the best middle school. I began studying all the time and somehow passed the exam, squeezing by with the lowest possible score allowed. A few years later, I repeated this feat to get into Beijing's top high school. I shocked everyone in my family constellation who thought I was not very ambitious or smart.

Right around this time, life was getting better in China, especially because Mao had died in 1976 and the years since his death had brought us some relief from his torturous regime. The new government had begun slowly opening the country up to the West. This initiated a vague sense of freedom in China. The Chinese people could dream of big things again.

John Shen (2nd from left) with other students at Peking University

My drive to change my life became stronger. In 1988, when I completed high school, I decided that I absolutely had to get accepted into Peking University Law School, the top university in China. My studying law was my parents' choice, but like all young Chinese people, I obeyed their wishes.

First Life-Changing Event

Everything in my life up to this point seemed picture-perfect. In 1989, my freshman year at Peking University Law School, I was respected as one of the top students. My goal was set on becoming a leading lawyer in Beijing, lifting my family out of our mediocre social status. We would join the ranks of prestigious families in this new blossoming and semi-capitalistic China.

Chairman Mao and Life in China under Communism

Mao Zedong (a.k.a. Chairman Mao) founded the People's Republic of China in 1949 and led it until his death in 1976. He is often considered as a great but ruthless leader who transformed China from a culturally backward and economically poor country to an industrial power capable of competing with advanced Western nations. He was Chairman of the Chinese Communist Party (CCP), which governed China with an iron fist under a revolutionary Marxist-Leninist philosophy, inciting class struggle and persecuting not just the wealthy, but also intellectuals and dissidents of any kind. His Great Leap Forward program, begun in 1958, sought to transition China from farming to mass industrialization, but it led to the starvation of an estimated 55 million people between 1958 and 1962. His Cultural Revolution, begun in 1966, created a campaign to persecute and imprison millions of people and led to untold brutality and executions.

The years of the 1960s and into the 1970s until his death were times of social chaos, economic instability, and political power struggles between Mao and his cadre of ministers. The student-led paramilitary group known as the Red Guard was tasked with eradicating the "Four Olds" (meaning old customs, old habits, old culture, and old ideas). Marching through China, they destroyed books, art museums, temples, shrines, and other sites of former Chinese culture. The Red Guards were also sent out to attack those whom they perceived as having "bourgeois values" and counter-revolutionary leanings.

Having been born in 1970, I was fortunate to be alive during only the six final years of Chairman Mao's stranglehold on China. However, his dictatorial and authoritarian legacy largely lived on through my childhood and teenage years, casting a shadow over my motivation to pursue a better life in China.

My dream was shattered by bullets and tanks in the spring of that year. The opening of the Chinese economy to market forces had inspired students at my university and dozens of other schools in China to demand better economic opportunities as well as democratic reforms. Student protests spilled out onto the streets in April. I participated in a hunger strike, believing our fasting could influence China's newest brutal and corrupt leaders.

The Chinese Communist Party, feeling too threatened to agree to student demands, instead sent 300,000 soldiers to Beijing. Armored tanks rolled down the streets to come face to face with a group of brave students in Tiananmen Square. Our momentary revolution ended with the government's forces indiscriminately shooting live bullets, massacring hundreds of student protestors and bystanders. Thousands more were wounded. It was a bloody day, one that remains in world history as one of the worst government repressions ever.

Famous photo of a lone protestor facing down
the column of tanks sent to quash the student protests

This tragedy became a driving force in my life. I realized that I could no longer live in China. Before I completed my four years at Peking University Law School and graduated, I knew I had to leave my homeland. I decided to apply to graduate school in the United States and seek out the American Dream, though I did not truly understand what it would take. But in my view, just as in the eyes of millions of immigrants throughout the world, the US appeared to be the most open society and the most technologically advanced. Who would not want to live in that place?

Not Easy to Get Out of China

Like immigrants throughout the world whose lives are uprooted by war, political repression, civil unrest, poverty, and zero opportunities for freedom, I set my sights on getting a full scholarship at the best American university that would accept me as soon as possible. I no longer wanted to practice law; my new ambition was to get a PhD in sociology.

To get out of China in 1992, you could not just buy a plane ticket and fly away, because the government required many steps to exit the country. Not only did my family have insufficient money for airfare to the US, but the only way I could afford the cost of an American graduate school was to win a *full* scholarship, which meant both free tuition and full living expenses.

I had begun applying to dozens of American graduate programs in the spring of my senior year at law school. There were no computers available to the average Chinese person at that time. I had to go to a library to read the printed catalog published by each US school.

My applications that year won free tuition to a few schools, but not living expenses. I knew that those offers were not enough for me to get a visa and had to turn them all down. Without any options, I took a job as a paralegal in a Beijing law firm until the next academic year—I could barely wait.

I was magnetically driven to leave China and move to the US. Every weekend, I worked on the applications and my entrance essays. I sent more than 20 applications; this time I won 11 full financial aid offers in either fellowships or assistantships, including offers from Princeton University and Duke University. I chose Duke because they admitted me before Princeton offered and had all the qualities I was looking for in a new life.

Perkins Library and Rubinstein Library at Duke University in Durham, NC

John Shen

Back in the spring of 1993, my acceptance at 11 schools set a record in Beijing. All of sudden I became well known in the community of students applying for US colleges. I was invited to give talks to other students and families who were applying for admission and scholarships abroad. I found myself speaking in the main auditorium at the National Library in Beijing to over 1,000 people, highlighting how I managed this success. The impact was beyond my imagination; in subsequent years, I met many students in the US who, I found out, had attended my presentation and been motivated by what I achieved. I know my success derived from having a strong internal drive to change my life.

But going to the US was still not certain, even with a 100% fully paid fellowship. The Chinese Communist Party believed they had a right to control who leaves the country and put out two absurd mandates in the early 1990s:

- First, I had to prove that I had a relative (defined by the "Six Categories of Qualified Relatives" in the Party's policy) living anywhere outside of China, other than my brother who was in the US. Of course, this requirement made no sense for students trying to study outside of China, but I was fortunate to discover a distant relative living in Taiwan to fulfill it.

- Secondly, I had to pay 10,000 Yuan to the government, a fortune by my family's standards. My parents borrowed money from many family members to send me to America. I would be indebted to them for their generosity and could not fail them.

First Years in the United States

In the summer of 1993, I arrived in Los Angeles, where my older brother had moved. He was nine years older and had gotten out of China in the summer of 1989, when it was easier. He was teaching Chinese at Pomona College, and I was to stay with him for a short time before going to Duke in North Carolina. Exiting LAX airport, I experienced a sudden culture shock. For a 23-year-old Chinese student, the transition from Beijing to Los Angeles was like arriving at another planet, one even more civilized than Earth. At that time, China had no supermarkets, no freeways, and almost no freedom of movement. I was enthralled with America.

When I finally arrived at Duke a few weeks later, I believed I was in paradise. The Duke University campus was a garden of delights for me. The campus was more beautiful than any university I had ever imagined, with Georgian architecture on the East Campus and Gothic architecture on the West Campus. I was assigned to live in an on-campus two-bedroom apartment with another graduate student, a fellow from Germany. I studied constantly. In those first few months my childhood habit of daydreaming fed my mind vivid images of the day I would proudly graduate, having earned my American PhD.

But sometimes your drive towards a goal suffers a serious setback. By the end of my first year at Duke, I realized a career in sociology was not what I wanted to do with my life. One night as I was reading the *American Journal of Sociology*, an academic journal that included job ads from colleges and universities across the US, it suddenly became clear that there would be few career opportunities for me in that field. I became worried and frustrated. I loved being in North Carolina and refused to return to China. I would have to change my life's plans yet again.

My drive to find another way to remain in the US led to me to transfer into Duke's master's program in statistics and decision sciences. I had become quite good at math and logic and, at this point in my life, I was driven to be career oriented. Looking back, this transition was clearly the spark behind my decision to become a businessman—and eventually an entrepreneur. It was a pivotal event that determined the remaining arc of my life.

Luck, Skill, or Both?

Six months before my expected graduation in May 1996 with a master's degree in statistics and decision sciences, I started a job search. I could not afford to wait for the actual graduation day for an indisputable reason: as a foreign student on an F-1 student visa, if I did not have a job within two months of finishing Duke, my visa to stay in America would expire and I would be forced to leave the country.

I frequently went to the career office at Duke, which helped me set up a number of job interviews with on-campus recruiters representing many American companies. Based on my résumé, I also was invited to be interviewed at the headquarters of several major companies, including AT&T and Capital One. I was optimistic and hopeful.

Like many foreign students though, I was at a deficit compared to American graduates. Despite my impending degree, I was like an alien from another planet. My English was accented and still somewhat broken, and worst of all, I was still introverted, shy, and very Chinese in my cultural outlook. In my job interviews, I must have appeared too reserved and unambitious to employers seeking extroverted go-getters. They could not see my internal ambition to work hard and achieve the American Dream. I had no network of people who could help me find a job.

After graduation, as the two-month deadline for my visa ticked away, I became increasingly worried that I would be forced to leave the country. Approaching the very last day of my ticking time bomb, I retreated to my bedroom in the house I shared with other graduate students. I felt overwhelmed and emotionally distraught as I considered my predicament. If I returned to Beijing, I would be a failure, having wasted my time earning a graduate degree for nothing. I would disappoint my parents and many others family members who had loaned me the money to study in the US. They were counting on me to succeed.

Life felt so hopeless that I sat on the carpet and began to cry until I fell asleep.

The next morning, I awoke on the floor to the sound of one of my roommates yelling up to me from downstairs. "There's a phone call for you," he screamed. I descended the stairs, red-eyed and with a cloudy head. I grabbed the phone and weakly said, "Hello." It was the manager of a consulting company in Kalamazoo, Michigan. I had met him months ago in one of my on-site interviews. The company had invited me to fly there to interview for a possible job, which I did, but they decided that I was not qualified for the position. As I left the interview, the manager said, reassuringly, "If something comes up, I'll be in touch." Of course, I believed it was just a courtesy phrase to reject a candidate nicely.

But now, on the phone, this manager asked me if I would be interested in a different job the firm had to offer. He insisted that I had the necessary skills for it. Interestingly, this manager was also an immigrant; he was from Africa and had gone to the University of Nebraska for his master's degree. I have no doubt he understood the special challenges we immigrants face in landing jobs.

My life was saved! I soon packed everything in a small suitcase and moved to Kalamazoo, where my employer assigned me to work as a project consultant for clients that needed statistical research. I spent six months at the end of 1996 in that small town, including a winter from hell, with record-setting snow for seven days in a row that piled higher than my car. My company then sent me to live in Chicago to work on projects with GE and the Rush Cancer Institute. A year later, I joined another company and moved to Indianapolis for a long-term project with Eli Lilly and Company.

With this experience, my skills as a consultant had become extremely valuable and I was courted by a company in Philadelphia to come join them. By now, I had married and we were expecting our first baby; but the new job fascinated me, so I accepted it and we moved to Philly.

Over the next five years, I thrived and moved up the ranks at this company, eventually becoming a department head. I loved being in Philly and was starting to feel that I belonged in America.

Downtown Kalamazoo in snow—view from Arcadia Creek playground

Becoming an American

Before continuing with the story of my journey to become an entrepreneur, you must understand that the drive of an immigrant in America to create a business is completely limited by the US laws regarding the immigration process. Immigrants who are allowed to come to the US as students have an F-1 visa, and as stated above, upon graduation, they must obtain a job within a two-month grace period or else they must return to their country.

The problem is, getting a job requires finding a company that is willing to "sponsor" you, meaning they attest that they need your skills, and they have to prove they could not find a US citizen or permanent resident to fill the position offered to you. The employer must eventually file a time-consuming green card application that, if approved, allows you to permanently work in the US. But in the interim, the employer must also sponsor a work visa called H-1B. The bigger problem in the last 25 years is, the total number of the H-1B visas has been far from sufficient for the number of foreigners applying, so only some of these petitions can be approved in the annual H-1B lottery.

The initial H-1B visa is good for only three years, and then renewable for an additional three years. During these six years, you can begin applying for a green card, which gives you permanent residency and the right to work, but it can take this entire amount of time or more to get approved. Meanwhile, you get a work permit but you must work full-time for that sponsoring employer during that period. As you might imagine, there are some potential negative consequences for you if your employer chooses to take advantage of the rules; for instance, keeping your salary low, knowing you cannot leave. The worst limitation of the H-1B visa process is that you cannot start your own business, no matter how much drive you have, until you have a green card.

This limitation was a big element in my journey to become an entrepreneur. After my graduation, I spent the first year at my first employer in a practical training status. After my second employer filed an H-1B petition in 1997, due to the shortage of the visas, I was forced to leave the job without pay for three months before I finally received my H-1B visa. Then I used almost all six years of the H-1B visa to obtain my green card. In those seven years, I was unable to start my own business.

In 2002, I was finally reaching the very last phase of the green card application. This phase of the process normally takes only a year to receive a final approval, but I heard nothing. I made frequent inquiries through my attorney as to the status of my application, but we never received any meaningful response. Two years went by and I was fearing that something happened and I would never receive an approval on my green card application.

I was frustrated and worried that I would have to leave the United States for China. It felt like a repetition of the experience I had at Duke, when I graduated and needed to find a job and had only days left before I would have been forced to leave the country. My hope was waning and it felt like the government was saying I do not belong in the US.

Finally, I took action of my own. I called one of the Pennsylvania senators, describing my ordeal and asking his office for help. I was told to write a letter to explain the situation and I mailed the letter to the senator's office. Once again I got no reply. However, a month later, I received a letter from the United States Citizenship and Immigration Services (USCIS) asking me to come in and redo my fingerprints. In the envelope was my letter to the senator in his envelope. In other words, the senator's office had done nothing other than to put my letter to them into their own envelope and forward it to USCIS. The mere fact that my letter came from the senator's office had finally dislodged the bureaucratic logjam. I later found out that USCIS could easily lose some pending applications. My application, whatever happened to it, was not on track until the senator's forwarding of my letter made USCIS spend some time searching for it. I had started the process in 1997 and finally in 2004 I received my green card. My case is typical for many foreign students trying to obtain a green card.

The immigration system in the US is stacked against highly motivated immigrants who have exceptional drive and intellect. Many of them want to become entrepreneurs, but they are required to spend a great deal of time obtaining their permanent residency before they can launch a company. They may come here as students with the American Dream and get their first jobs and patiently wait the years and years it takes to get their green card. But I have seen many talented people get jobs out of college and then be unable to get their green card because the process took so much time they lost their H-1B status and had to leave. It makes me wonder how many smart, creative, and highly motivated immigrants give up on being entrepreneurs, after waiting too long to act on their ideas and drive. I wonder how much talent the US misses out on through a bureaucratic immigration system that needs to be fixed.

The immigration system in the US is stacked against highly motivated immigrants who have exceptional drive and intellect.

John Shen

Paying Back My Appreciation for Duke University

Duke has long been a big part of my life. When I completed my master's degree in 1996, I was grateful for all I had come to learn at this wonderful institution. Despite my difficult times as a foreign student, I was thankful for my experience and I eventually wanted to give something back.

In 2009, I volunteered to serve on the Alumni Admissions Advisory Committee (AAAC), which supports the undergraduate admission process by interviewing applicants from all over the world. Since I was traveling to China often during this period of time for my company ALC (discussed in the next chapter), I worked for AAAC China a lot, interviewing many prospective students throughout China. In 2013, I became the Chair of the AAAC China.

By 2015, I had performed so much service for the university and interviewed so many students, I was awarded the "Forever Duke Award," a prestigious honor given only to a few individuals each year. I am currently still Chair of the AAAC China team, continuing to assist Duke as the university selects the top students from all of China for admittance to its undergraduate program in North Carolina. I have traveled many times to China in that capacity, helping representatives from Duke's admissions department as they visit high schools, attend college admissions fairs, and deliver critical information to prospective students and their families. I always tell students how much Duke changed my life and gave me an entirely new sense of how to live.

To show my gratitude, I also started giving back financially. In 2017, I established a unique endowment fund to support the school's recruitment of students from developing countries. I am proud of this effort, not only because the fund is unprecedented in Duke's history, but because, having been a student there 30 years ago, I am committed to helping international students who struggle to find the resources to attend this great university.

My Entrepreneurial Drive Kicks In

My desire to live the American Dream was in high gear by this time, or so I thought . . . until my internal drive threw me a curve ball. It was around 2002 that I began to look at my future and wonder, *Is this all there is?* I could picture myself all the way to my retirement and what I saw was frightening. I would be doing the exact same work for decades. It was not exciting to me, spending the rest of my life doing statistical analyses and programming. The work and lifestyle did not seem very special; in fact, I was bored.

Meanwhile, I had taken my family on vacation to Disney World in Orlando, Florida a couple times. Surviving the cold Philly winter required at least one week of sunshine each February or March, and having kids required treating them to the Disney experience, of course. On these trips to Florida, I heard about many investors buying properties to rent out to tourists short-term. I thought the idea sounded brilliant and decide to go for it. I purchased a vacation house as a rental property for my own investment.

When you are driven, you can be surprised at how you view opportunities. I decided that to manage my one rental house, I had to learn how to master the property rental business. I began spending time putting my Orlando house up for rent on many rental websites. I recruited an eager young guy named James to help me, who many years later became a successful real estate professional in the Orlando area. Together we started a property management company that arranged for the cleaning and maintenance of the house. Then my neighbors in Philadelphia began asking me about my investment, so I started to teach a few of them how to do it. I introduced them to the real estate agent I had used and also to my property management company for their purchases. Many of them also bought houses and began making money by renting them out.

When you are driven,

you can be

surprised at how

you view

opportunities.

The Entrepreneurial Flash

Suddenly the thought of becoming an entrepreneur and changing my life again solidified in my mind. It felt like the logical culmination of my entire life. The former shy Beijing student who could not speak English was just a ghost of my past. I was now as much a go-getting American businessman as anyone raised in America. Super-sizing the American Dream became my new fantasy. I realized that I could earn the money others made. I could get into real estate and do everything my agent and property management company were doing.

I studied and quickly passed the real estate exam, earning a license in Florida. I joined a real estate company and began selling houses in Orlando on weekends, while keeping my regular job. After working Monday to Friday as a full-time employee, I would fly people I knew—friends, neighbors, acquaintances from everywhere—to Florida on Friday night and spend the weekend selling them properties. My business grew quickly.

I could not stop the entrepreneurial train at this point. In 2004, I obtained a broker's license, which extended my abilities to perform transactions in the real estate business. Going one step further, I also started traveling to many major cities in America to present this opportunity, bringing hundreds of interested buyers to central Florida hunting for short-term rental properties such as the ones I bought for myself. I found myself doing weekend seminars in New York, Washington, D.C., Boston, Chicago, San Francisco, Los Angeles, San Diego, and any other cities where I could prospect investment property buyers.

The real estate boom in 2003 became so strong that my businesses in Florida kicked into high gear. I began living two lives: one, that of an employee; the other, that of a real estate entrepreneur. The one that I put my heart and soul into was the life of an entrepreneur. It was not the money that pulled me towards this; it was an inner drive to create something of my own that would be life-changing.

FIRST-GENERATION ENTRPRENEURS: SPECIAL ISSUES REGARDING DRIVE

If you are not a first-generation immigrant, it may be difficult for you to comprehend the strength of drive that immigrants to the United States have. We are unlike other Americans who, being born in the US, assume that they have the freedom to do whatever they want in life. Many natural-born Americans have the ambition to start their own business, but I believe their drive is different than that of first-generation immigrants.

Immigrants to America often come from countries that have no freedom. They may have had very little opportunity for a good education. Their government may not believe in capitalism and thus not allow anyone to dream of running their own business. They may have come from poor families with no resources to even start a business. For such immigrants, coming to the US is the first time in their lives that they can actually release their ambitions. They have no limiting beliefs to hold them back anymore. Here they not only can dream, but they can act on their dreams. They can get good jobs; they can even start their own business if they want to.

Some immigrants, like me, come to the US to further our university education—and then we simply do not want to return to our native land because that would be going back to an environment we can no longer tolerate.

Another commonality among first-generation immigrants who wish to remain in the US is that they all face the tough challenge of getting a green card; a green card and permanent residency for themselves are both necessary before an immigrant can even start a business. As described earlier in the chapter, my personal struggle to obtain my green card was typical; immigrants face a very long and arduous process. In my case, I had to find an employer who was willing to vouch for me so I could stay in the country for up to the six years that it could take to go through the green card process. This stressful process is why many immigrants come away from their green card experience with a strong drive to succeed, given all they have been through to remain in the States. They are so appreciative of the opportunity to be here and to have the freedoms afforded to American citizens.

The point is, for many immigrants it is almost impossible to plan their future when they have no idea if they even have a future in the US. When it comes down to career development, what often happens is that this difficult immigration process puts a damper on the entrepreneurial dreams that many immigrants have—until the moment they finally receive their green card. And when they can finally breathe fresh air, nothing can possibly stop them any longer.

The natural human drive to create one's own life becomes very powerful for ambitious immigrants. The forces that drive immigrants to become entrepreneurs can be very deeply rooted in the deprivation of their youth, or in the extreme lengths they must go to in order to live and work in the US—or both. As well, many immigrants literally have "no option" to go back to where they came from, and that is why they will work harder and longer than people whose lives afforded them unlimited options. When you have no options, you are propelled forward because there is no other choice. You must succeed.

John Shen

REFLECTIONS

Consider these questions. Write out your answers or identify a "success buddy" such as a business partner, another entrepreneur, or a spouse or friend with whom you can discuss the questions.

- How driven are you? On a scale of 1 to 10, with 10 being the highest, what number would you ascribe to your internal drive?

- Can you pinpoint when you developed your drive? In childhood? As a teenager? Was it due to any specific event or a person who inspired you? Reflect on this and acknowledge how it changed your life. Does thinking of that event or person still affect your drive forward?

- What does your drive propel you to do? Are you driven to invent, innovate, or initiate a new business?

- Are you a tire-kicker, always thinking about entrepreneurship but not taking the jump? Or are you ready to make the sacrifices necessary to be an entrepreneur?

- How high are you seeking to jump? What are your goals? Do you want to be a well-known entrepreneur cited in the media or a civic-minded entrepreneur involved in local or national politics?

CHAPTER 2

Ability to Capitalize on Opportunities

CAPITALIZE

- To infuse a business with cash

- To take a risk in order to gain advantage from opportunities

- Synonyms: exploit, profit from

John Shen

In using the term "capitalize" as the second talent you need to succeed as an entrepreneur, I am referring to the ability to recognize opportunities, jump on them, and use them to your business advantage. Perhaps some people naturally know how to exploit situations, like having intuition or a "sixth sense." But I believe every hard-working, thoughtful entrepreneur can develop this talent. I did.

The art of "capitalizing" on opportunities is inherently related to "capitalism" as an economic system. Capitalism requires freedom for individuals to control their own business, take their own risks, and earn their own profits. Capitalist enterprises need to be funded to pay for their startup costs until a profit can be made. Capitalist entrepreneurs need to be able to capitalize on opportunities to promote their new product or service, sell it to customers, and generate profits with which to pay themselves and their employees, and to invest in growing the business.

As my parents were educators, not shopkeepers or businesspeople, I had little knowledge of business or how to run a company. Having been born in a country that did not even allow capitalism for the entire 20th century and still barely tolerates it in this 21st century, I had no significant education in how to identify opportunities to grow a business. In essence, I had no training in how to look at trends and recognize when one might become a profitable business.

The success I had in capitalizing on the real estate market in Florida is why I say that any entrepreneur can understand capitalization and how to do it. Here is my story of how I learned to jump on an opportunity that I believed was worth every ounce of my intellect and energy. This is the real start of what I have come to call my "Entrepreneurship 1.0" phase in life.

My Strange Double Life

CORPORATE EMPLOYEE VS. ENTREPRENEUR

My budding real estate business, consisting of my broker business and my property management company, was booming by 2003. But the entrepreneurial spark had now become a flame. I saw an enormous opportunity looking squarely at me. It occurred to me that in Orlando I had tapped only a miniscule portion of the enormous potential market of investors who might want to purchase Florida homes to live in or rent out. Millions of Americans all across the country could be prospective investors. All I had to do was reach out to them. If they were not coming to me, I would go to them.

Only once in my life had I ever spoken to a large audience of people—it was back in Beijing when I had won the 11 scholarships and was asked to go onstage and speak to audiences who seemed to be inspired by what I achieved. Back then, I spoke to over 1,000 people in the National Library in Beijing and I did well. I thought to myself, *If I did it back then, I can do it again now.*

I decided that the only way to capitalize on the gold mine of the Florida housing market that I saw in front of me was to create a dazzling presentation and take it across the country. Yes, I founded one of those "real estate investment seminars"—the kind that you may have seen advertised on TV in the past where the presenter stands in front of hundreds of people and explains how they can make a lot of money in real estate. These seminars were (and still are) popular because they offer free instructions on how to invest in real estate and make a profit, just as I was doing in Orlando. To capitalize on the popularity of those kinds of programs, I began traveling to New Jersey and parts of New York on Friday nights, after my regular job, with my real estate seminar presentation.

Soon, my appetite grew for a wider audience. I decided to try selling Florida properties in California. I would take a flight on Friday evening to San Francisco or Los Angeles, arrive late at night, get up Saturday morning to give my presentation to crowds of investors and do the same on Sunday in another location, then take a red-eye flight back to Philly Sunday night, and land early Monday morning, where I would go to the men's room at the airport, change for work, and show up at my office promptly at 8:30 a.m.—in time to begin the week as a full-time employee at my day job.

For months, no one in the office suspected that I had this alternative life as an entrepreneur. After about six months, though, my boss noticed that I was "a very busy man" and sensed that I had another job beyond my work hours. One time he was joking about the fact that I appeared to be getting gray hair. He chided me, "John, you probably work too hard." Fortunately, he did not make an issue out of it, since my work performance was still impeccable. I got the impression he respected my ambition and drive.

However, I was no doubt struggling to schedule and complete everything that I had to cover in my own business in the evenings and over the weekends. One can only do so much. In the meantime, I could not continue my normal life; I had to sacrifice many family duties as a young father due to my time constraints.

When Is It Time to Face Reality?

A PATH TO ENTREPRENEURSHIP

Many entrepreneurs must initially do what I had to do to build a business—live the double life of working a job while running a startup venture. When you do this, the drive to succeed needs to be strong. If it is not, you can be tempted to abandon your entrepreneurial endeavor and just walk away. When things become too challenging, it can feel easier to stick with your salaried job and let go of your dream. If you are in this situation, or predicament, let me encourage you to keep going as long as you can.

Many entrepreneurs must initially do what I had to do to build a business— live the double life of working a job while running a startup venture.

John Shen

Starting a business takes self-discipline, stamina, strength, and conviction. These are all traits necessary for creating a business and sticking with it long enough to capitalize on those opportunities you believe will lead to a sustainable venture. The risk factor weighs on you heavily. The investment of time is that not only of hours and weeks, but of months, if not years. As well, you will be financing it with your own funds or borrowing from others. This is why maintaining your drive is critical to successful entrepreneurship.

I led my double life for about a year, between 2003 and 2004. It was both exhilarating and exhausting. I was away from my family every weekend, giving presentations somewhere in the US. I worked my job 9:00 to 5:00 Monday through Friday, then stayed at the office a few hours more to make phone calls to check in and manage my staff in Orlando. My stress began to grow, of course, but I was too driven to let it defeat me. I persevered.

Eventually, I had to face reality. Despite being well paid by my day-job company, I preferred my entrepreneurial real estate business more than my regular job. On a Friday, I approached my boss and informed him of my decision to leave the company. He reacted by pleading with me to stay. He told me in confidence the company would soon go public and my career would easily take off as the company was growing. Then he looked at me sternly and said, "Sit down here and think about it." He left the room and . . . I heard him lock the door. He was that serious about forcing me to stay. I was locked in his office for a couple of hours. Of course, when he returned he asked, "Have you changed your mind?" But I had not. I knew I had a future in real estate that I could develop into a wealth-building, sustainable business—and I had accomplished it all myself.

Eighteen years later, one of my employees came to me as the CEO of the company and proposed the same idea to me. She was determined to leave her job with me to build her own business. Prior to that moment, like my former employer, I already knew she was busy developing her own business beyond regular work hours, but I had remained tolerant. When she spoke out, I wanted to confirm one thing with her. I asked, "Are you ready to take on the challenge of being an entrepreneur?" She said yes.

I sensed her desire was like mine back in 2004. The conversation only took about two minutes. I did not lock her in my office but wished her well immediately. To my surprise, she told me a secret—what motivated her to pursue an entrepreneurial career was actually my life. She had learned a great deal from me over the years and felt confident that she would be able to run a business by herself. I was happy to hear this, although it seemed like I had planted the seeds to undermine the operation of my own company.

Capitalizing on More Opportunities

I moved my family from Philadelphia to Orlando in late 2004 so I could blast ahead full speed growing my business. My entrepreneurial endeavor in real estate began performing beyond expectations. I had more clients buying homes from me than many established agents who had been in the Orlando real estate business years before me. I was like the proverbial dog chasing a car and unexpectedly catching it, so I had to act.

To capture every angle of the real estate business, I soon obtained a license to become a mortgage broker and opened my own office. This gave me the trifecta of customer services for anyone investing in a home in Orlando: real estate agent, mortgage broker, and property management company. I could do it all for my client investors.

With the sums of money I was earning, I realized that I could capitalize on one more element of the real estate business that I did not yet have—land development. Florida was booming with an influx of young couples seeking a less expensive state in which to live, as well as retirees desiring to spend their final decades in a year-round warm climate. Developers were buying raw, uninhabited land everywhere around Orlando. They would put in the infrastructure and then sell the parcels to builders or even individual investors who would apply to the county for a permit to build a residential property.

I didn't have the millions of dollars in funds to buy the land and build an entire housing development myself, speculating on selling every home. But I had enough money to buy a large parcel of raw land, or many parcels, with the infrastructure already in place. I began purchasing prime parcels and resold them, many for communities of homes.

The Boom Years

TOO UNBELIEVABLE TO BELIEVE

The years of 2005 and 2006 were extraordinary in the Florida real estate business. The state led the US in home sales and land investments. At that time, mortgage rates had dipped very low, and bank requirements to buy a home were so relaxed that anyone could purchase a house with barely 5% down, sometimes even 0% down. Banks had broadly relaxed the requirements to obtain a mortgage, handing out no-cost (no points, no fees) home loans to just about anyone who claimed they had a job and an income, no verified proof needed. These loans had a very low "teaser" rate for the first year, which would then bump up to a higher interest rate in the next and succeeding

years. With just a signature, nearly anyone breathing could purchase a home selling for $200,000 or higher. This is the famous "subprime" issue that generated a huge real estate bubble. When this bubble burst in 2007, the crash of the entire banking system of the US triggered the financial crisis in 2008.

Those two years were magical for Americans wanting to buy a home. Hundreds of thousands of people were able to purchase rather expensive homes far beyond what their incomes allowed, expecting to flip them (resell them) within the one-year teaser low-interest rate time frame so they could profit from the fast-rising home prices. Even the woman working for the janitorial company that cleaned my office owned several houses.

Meanwhile, property values were correspondingly skyrocketing. The Florida market was hotter than anywhere else in the country. Every month, home and land prices went up. Here is a real story: My reputation spread as a powerful buyer's agent who produced lots of qualified buyers. I often brought in 200 to 300 buyers for any properties or land that became available.

Being considered one of just a few top brokers in the Orlando area, one Monday I received an email from a large builder, inviting me to bring buyers to his office on the following Thursday. The email said he was scheduled to release some new properties (lots with building plans). The email had been sent to only three brokers. I shared that information with many of my clients, hoping to seize that opportunity.

But on Wednesday, I received a phone call from the builder, telling me that the new properties were already "GONE." I found out later that the day after the builder sent out the first email, hundreds of buyers had come to his office, even camping outside in tents and sleeping bags to wait for the opening bid moment on Thursday. The camps had become so crowded that the builder could no longer manage it. He had no choice but to quickly sell the properties to the first few campers—two days ahead of time. What a crazy market!

How to Capitalize on Trends

Over the years I have developed my own ways to capitalize on opportunities and trends. I maintain that anyone can learn to recognize where there may be a business idea that you can capitalize on. Here are some recommendations that come from my experience.

1. While you are a busy entrepreneur trying to run your venture, you need to make time at least once a month to do some homework, scouting out anything that might affect your business. I try to do a monthly Sunday breakfast with my wife and business partners to discuss what is going on in our industry and beyond. It helps me see new opportunities.

2. Watch headline news related to Congress and governments. Any new legislation or policy change can generate interesting new market demands and therefore possibly inspire ideas for new products or services. When things are happening that are traumatic, there are always policy changes. The easy way to track these is to read a quick summary of the legislation and pick out the key points, though sometimes that is not enough. If you want to fully take advantage of new legislation, you may need to read it all and find a particular section that relates to your industry. You can often catch some interesting policy changes that will create new trends.

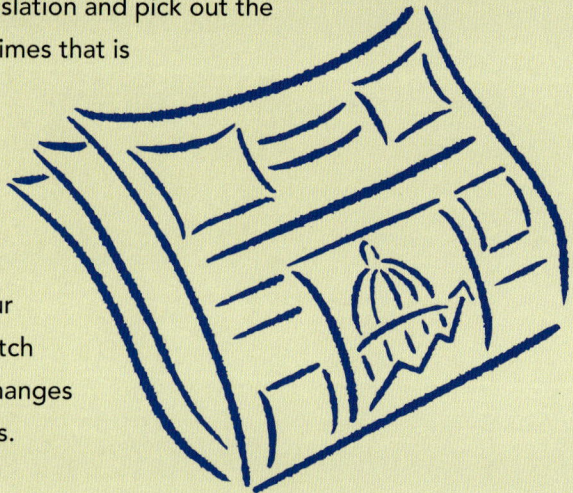

3. Peruse the professional journals and magazines in your field. Look for trend reports or unique events that strike you as being new and noteworthy.

4. Pay attention to social media and see who the influencers are in your industry. What are they saying?

5. Go to conferences or expos to learn what is available in the market and what is expected to come out.

6. Talk to your customers and pay attention to any shifts in their views. If they are buying from competitors, ask why.

7. Maintain regular communications with professionals in other business sectors. Focus on people you do not work with. I found it to be very helpful to learn from them because they are often people who can help you think out of the box, whereas the people around you are in the same box as you. The thoughts of outsiders can often spur new ideas and concepts that help you improve your existing products or services.

8. Volunteer your services to give something back to your community. You can often meet people from many walks of life who can enhance your perceptions of problems, your thinking style, and your skills as a leader.

Watching for Signs of Trouble

To capitalize successfully on opportunities, entrepreneurs must keep their attention focused on both present conditions and future trends. Once you get started in your venture, you have to look ten feet in front of you as well as peer out over the horizon line. Does your product or service meet the market conditions at this time? Will it continue to meet market needs in the coming six months? One year? Three years?

Sometimes you can spot the signs of changing conditions; if so, you need to begin taking steps to mitigate your risks or even save your business. When an avalanche occurs, if you look up, you may find out in which direction you should run. If you don't look up, you are not aware of it, and you lose the last opportunity to protect yourself. In 2006, I made the huge mistake of not recognizing the avalanche called the real estate crash occurring on the horizon.

Depending on your age, you may or may not be old enough to recall how the US housing bubble began to blow up towards the end of 2006. By this time, several years of buyer demand had driven home prices up to unsustainable levels. The low "teaser rate" one-year variable mortgage loans were now expiring, bumping up the interest rate for thousands of homeowners to a "normal" monthly payment they could no longer afford.

In Q3 of 2006, banks began to see thousands of foreclosures throughout Florida, as people could no longer pay their mortgage. This led to declining prices because so many homes became available for purchase—the basic principle of supply and demand. Meanwhile, banks began tightening the income and employment documentation requirements for mortgage loans, given how many bad loans they had already made.

To capitalize successfully on

opportunities, entrepreneurs

must keep their attention focused

on both present conditions

and future trends. Once you get

started in your venture,

you have to look ten feet

in front of you as well as peer out

over the horizon line.

My entrepreneurial empire consisted of nothing but real estate-related companies. By 2007, fewer and fewer people were buying homes in Orlando, so my real estate agent business slackened. As a mortgage broker, not a mortgage lender, my company was not on the hook for abandoned loans associated with mortgage foreclosures. But with no one buying homes, I could not earn any brokerage fees. In the meantime, I had zero applications to process in my mortgage broker business, and thus no profit rolling into that business. I had sold my property management company before 2006 and therefore no longer had the last business that could have generated a stable cash flow when there were no new transactions to be made. I essentially did everything wrong in my business structure and dug a big hole for myself.

By mid-2007, all my businesses were in jeopardy, yet I had no way of regaining control. The economic trends for the entire real estate industry across the US were coalescing into a disastrous conclusion for the housing bubble. More than 2.2 million foreclosures occurred in 2007 alone.

The repercussions of this explosive downturn were spreading across the entire housing industry. In a domino effect, even homeowners who paid their mortgages responsibly were impacted. The declining home values made their mortgages sink "underwater," meaning their mortgage loan was greater than their property value. Who wants to keep paying off a mortgage loan of $500,000 when your home is valued at just $400,000? Many homeowners simply walked away from their property. Foreclosures and bankruptcies mounted day after day throughout the US, but Florida led the downward race.

What made my life so difficult was the fact that as a real estate professional with access to so many "good" deals, I had purchased many properties for myself. When the crash happened, I owned six homes. I was able to sell three smaller properties by the end of 2007, with zero profit, but could not sell the three big ones. All three big properties later went "underwater."

My Ultimate Crash

At the end of 2007, I was nearly broke. I was looking squarely at the complete failure of all my businesses. I soon experienced what no entrepreneur wants to face: I no longer had a way to make money. The entire real estate industry was in chaos. My businesses had no value in a sharply declining economy. My bank account was draining my savings like a sieve. Worse, mortgage rates had started to jump, so my mortgage bills on the three homes I owned went up to approximately $20,000 per month at the beginning of 2008. Without any income, I ran up all my credit cards to their limits before I inevitably had to cease payments. I was in serious default on all these mortgage loans.

I knew that I was going to lose all three homes I owned. In fact, over the next two years I sold two of them in short sales (meaning I sold them for less than the remaining mortgages due) and I lost the other to foreclosure. It was so painful to watch that happening but there was nothing I could do to stop it. As a father of two young kids and a husband whose wife did not work and depended solely on my income, I was everything that a total loser was all about. In 2009, my wife and I divorced. Even though the financial trouble was not the main reason for my divorce, it certainly was a factor.

In early 2008, the American economy collapsed. Despite the federal government's attempts to shore up the real estate industry with huge loans to banks and lowered interest rates, the housing market was critically wounded. Several large mortgage loan companies had already declared bankruptcy in 2007, with more following in the next year.

In January 2008, the stock market began sliding downwards; in March, it hit its lowest level since 2006, declining more than 20%. Lehman Brothers, the fourth largest investment bank in the country, filed for bankruptcy in September that year. From that point on, several years of economic hardship would descend on the US and throughout the world in what became known as the Great Recession.

Never Giving Up vs. Losing It All

In the summer of 2008, I hatched the only survival plan I could think of. I had a few parcels of land I had not yet been able to sell. I decided to fly to Honolulu, where I had formerly done presentations on buying

10,997.35

D: 03/05/09 O: 6,726.50 H: 6,979.22
L: 6,544.10 C: 6,594.52 V: 4,588,238,848

2-day bars History
June 19, 2013 14:21

Index

	Index
	12,612
	11,744
	10,876
	10,008
	9,140.0
	8,272.0
	7,404.0
	6,536.0
	5,668.0

2008 Crash

Volume

High Volume at the end of the Crash

High Volume at the beginning of the Recover

%

| May 2008 | Aug 2008 | Nov 2008 | Feb 2008 | May 2000 | Aug 2009 | Nove 2009 | Feb 2010 |

investment property in Florida. The Hawaiian real estate investment market was still hot, despite the start of the substantial recession on the mainland. For inexplicable reasons, many Hawaiian investors desired to own land in Florida. I had no choice anymore; I forced myself to make Hawaii my last stand.

I went back and forth between Florida and Hawaii several times that summer, pursuing a final push to make some money. In the meantime, it became clear to me that I had neither a reason to

80

maintain my office nor the funds to pay the rent or my employees. I told my staff they had to go. My office was in a beautiful three-story building in Champions Gate, less than 10 minutes from the main gate of Disney World and the other theme parks. It included seven spacious offices, a conference room, and everything else a professional office suite should have. The images of vacating all this are still painful to recall. I phoned a couple of friends to help me and we put everything that we could into our cars late in the evening . . . and just drove off. Effectively, I abandoned the lease, just as hundreds of bankrupt businesses had. It was a brutal shock to my pride and my ambition.

My nearly six years of hard work and the effort I had invested in building a profitable real estate "empire" and establishing a reputation as an Orlando business leader had vanished. Nothing I could do could save any of it. I had put all my eggs into the same basket—real estate—without any alternative income streams or Plan B to survive the Great Recession.

On what I expected to be my last trip to Hawaii, I arrived in Honolulu and met with some prospective investors. If I could capitalize on the opportunity to sell them my last few parcels, I would replenish my supply of funds and survive a while longer. I thought I might get lucky. Perhaps the recession would end sooner than later and I could revive my real estate business, as if nothing had happened.

My plan did not work. After a few days of trying to sell the parcels, I returned to my hotel room and stared out at the sun through the window of my room on the 16th floor. I opened the window and put my foot on the sill. As described in the opening to this book, I felt that I had completely failed and there was nothing to live for, no way to undo the mistakes I had made. The word "suicide" didn't cross my mind consciously, but that's exactly what I was facing. (In fact, several friends of mine—including a successful developer, an experienced property manager, and one investor—did commit suicide the following year, in 2009, the darkest year of the Great Recession.)

Of course, I did not take my own life. As described in this book's opening paragraphs, a bumped laptop that exposed an email I normally would have dismissed as spam essentially saved my life. After I read the story in that email, I closed the window and cried, just as I did on the night before I received my first job offer in Kalamazoo. The next day I awoke and returned to Florida, vowing to start anew.

The "Glass of Water" story in that fortuitous email opened my eyes to reframing how I perceived my problems. I was beyond lucky to read it before taking my life. That simple shift in perception changed the way I approached what I had assumed was an insurmountable set of obstacles. I realized how it was not all insurmountable; it was simply a challenge I had to overcome. I understood that we all face some type of pressure every day. But, as sentient, rational humans, we have the capacity to put any problem down in one single second. We can control our thoughts; we can prevent negative thinking and stress from distracting us from our ability to solve problems and get things done.

The "Glass of Water" story also saved me from taking a step that many entrepreneurs whose business fails believe they must do: file for bankruptcy. Inspired by the story to keep negative thinking from dominating my actions, I decided that I would keep marching forward to try to rebuild my credit and avoid the potential stigma of bankruptcy.

This lesson is important for all entrepreneurs, as you will have many dark moments. I encourage you to use the story of "A Glass of Water" as a touchstone that reminds you not to lose sight of your drive and your ability to capitalize on new opportunities.

We all face some type of pressure every day. But, as sentient, rational humans, we have the capacity to put any problem down in one single second. We can control our thoughts; we can prevent negative thinking and stress from distracting us from our ability to solve problems and get things done.

FIRST-GENERATION ENTREPRENEURS: SPECIAL ISSUES REGARDING FAILURE

No one likes to fail. But for many first-generation immigrants, the normal psychological feelings of failure—sadness, loss of self-esteem, anxiety, and depression—are compounded by the knowledge that you may have disappointed so many others who put their faith in your success in the United States. Your journey to come here may have been arduous and long, and yet you accepted the challenge. Parents and relatives may have loaned you money or supported your entry into the US. Some family members may have lived their life vicariously through you, so you may have a heavy feeling that your failure will hurt them personally. In effect, it can feel like the weight of the world is upon you.

While family members may be disappointed or even angry, recognize that you are the one who tried hard to succeed on their behalf. You are not to blame for things you cannot control. The antidote to failure is to remember that you probably learned a business lesson that you can use to start again. Keep in mind the "Glass of Water" story that shows how you can release the problem in a single second and refocus on creating new plans to try again.

REFLECTIONS

Consider these questions. Write out your answers or identify a "success buddy" such as a business partner, another entrepreneur, or a spouse or friend with whom you can discuss the questions.

- How well do you think you capitalize on opportunities? Is it a natural skill you have, or do you need to develop this talent?

- What opportunities might your entrepreneurial venture seek to profit from?

- What future trends do you need to follow to ensure your venture can survive?

- Are there any trends that are threatening your startup right now?

- What plans do you have to mitigate those threats?

- Do you follow the economic forecasts and are you prepared for a dip in the economy or even a mild or severe recession?

CHAPTER 3

Resilience

RESILIENCE

- The capacity to overcome difficulties quickly

- The property of a material to spring back into shape after being altered

- Synonyms: strength, toughness, recovery

John Shen

Many entrepreneurs experience total failure of their enterprises. Thousands of hopeful business owners launch an enterprise and make it work for a year or a few years, only to succumb eventually to poor cash flow, operational problems, staffing or management problems, or the overwhelming stress of running their business. Each year, even scores of high technology startups with millions of dollars of venture capital financing are unable to capitalize on the market they intended to conquer. They too go under because of poor strategic planning, ineffective leadership, overspending resources, or changes in market trends they had not predicted.

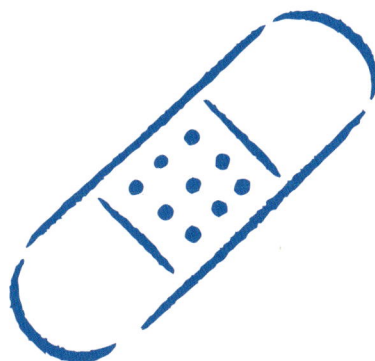

No entrepreneur is immune from failure. It can happen to the most experienced of businesspeople. Having resources is also not a guarantee against failure. You might make fewer mistakes when you have a lot of resources, but money does not protect against ineffective leadership or bad strategy. You can be extremely well funded and still fail.

Setbacks vs. Failure

The commonality among all entrepreneurs who fail is that they did not intend to fail. They began their enterprise with drive and ambition that pushed them to do everything possible to succeed. Their optimism and high hopes when they launched the business made them feel undefeatable. Their business plan was brilliant, their leadership team was brilliant, their product or service was going to attract more customers than they could handle, and their bank account would soon be full of cash. This was their reality . . . until the venture failed.

What I learned from my first experience of starting a business is that entrepreneurship is as much about dealing with setbacks and even overcoming outright failure as it is about learning how to achieve success. If you are going to be an entrepreneur, you will experience setbacks and failure; there is no doubt about it.

If you are going to be an entrepreneur, you will experience setbacks and failure; there is no doubt about it.

If you are skillful and lucky, you will face only setbacks, which I define as the daily snafus and unexpected twists and turns of events that force you to rethink some aspect of your business. Setbacks can happen at any time; you can have three or four on the same day. Some can be trivial and taken care of within hours, by letting go of the pressure in a single second and focusing your rational mind on solving the problems. Some setbacks are more substantial and can take weeks of effort to resolve.

Failure is, of course, more than a setback; it is a mortal wound. It means closing down your business, terminating your staff, vacating your office, and saying goodbye to suppliers and customers. After failure, many entrepreneurs lose their drive, then abandon any desire to start anew. The hard work, time away from family, the drain on their financial resources, and the stress of running the business are simply too overwhelming to try again.

The Top Reasons Why Businesses Fail

Many analysts cite a variety of reasons entrepreneurs fail. These are some of the most common ones.

- Failure to confirm a market for their product or service
- Not having a realistic business plan (or not following the one you have)
- Insufficient financing
- Failure to be agile and flexible in the face of changing trends
- Expanding too fast
- Lack of skilled leadership or inadequate management
- Overdependence on a few customers or a single product
- Ineffective marketing strategies
- Quitting too soon

Dealing with setbacks and outright business failure both require skills like creativity, agile thinking, flexibility, and stamina. But above these is what I consider the meta-talent at the foundation of entrepreneurial survival—*resilience*, the commitment to recover and keep trying.

Without resilience, the rest of the skills don't stand a chance. Without resilience, you cannot be creative or slip into agile thinking. Without resilience, you have no interest in being flexible, willing to "pivot" from the original plan that did not work to something that seems to be a better solution to the problem. Without resilience, it is difficult to maintain your stamina.

It is important to keep in mind that most successful entrepreneurial ventures take years to produce substantially profitable results. Given that setbacks are around the corner for any new venture, you need to be able to bounce back with another idea, another new venture.

And in the event that the worst case scenario occurs—impending failure—you need to be able to honestly and truthfully assess the cause of the failure, accept your responsibility, learn from the mistakes you made, and then gird yourself to try again.

Failure can be the best teacher. People seldom want to look for their own mistakes in the moments when they seem to control everything and are "on the rise." This quirk of human nature traps those who believe they are successful and always make the right decisions. The fact is, no one always makes the right decisions; everyone makes mistakes, here or there, and making money does not mean that your business is successful. If you are not aware of any mistakes you recently made, you are about to hit the wall, badly. In my case, prior to the real estate crash, I was always thinking that I was so successful and made all the right decisions. That error in thinking was a form of blindness; I could not tell what I might have done wrong.

When I was finally forced to go back to the starting line, I looked back and studied what went wrong. The lowest point of one's life can be the best moment to learn about oneself, especially figuring out one's weaknesses. That apparently happened to me. When I lost everything, I was forced to take a good hard look at all the components of the failure and realized one of the causes was my own way of thinking. I could now clearly see the many mistakes I had made in the past. I learned under what circumstances I could easily fail. This introspection helped me greatly after I launched ALC (American Lending Center) in 2009; so much so that I was able to stay away from the areas where I knew I could make the same mistakes again. When I was about to face similar challenges, I strategically found someone else—my business partners or employees—to handle them. I became smarter and was able to avoid my own weaknesses.

If your venture completely fails, as mine did in Florida, yet you have the resilience to keep being an entrepreneur, you will need to start the equivalent of another journey. Like me, you can look back on your first

Failure can be the best teacher. People seldom want to look for their own mistakes in the moments when they seem to control everything and are "on the rise." This quirk of human nature traps those who believe they are successful and always make the right decisions.

failed effort as your Entrepreneurship 1.0 journey. Your next attempt to launch a new venture becomes your Entrepreneurship 2.0 journey. Here's how mine happened.

You can look back on your first failed effort as your Entrepreneurship 1.0 journey. Your next attempt to launch a new venture becomes your Entrepreneurship 2.0 journey.

Hitting Rock Bottom

When I returned to Florida from Hawaii, I hit the second lowest point in my life (the lowest being my near suicide). I had little psychological strength and felt despondent and defeated. It was early 2009, and I basically had nothing. My bank account literally had just $7.00 in it. What else did I have? No paychecks anymore, the default mortgage and credit card accounts were the only things left.

That day, I stood outside a McDonalds and could not bring myself to go in and spend any of my precious $7.00. I went home and looked in the mirror. What I saw was the shell of the man I had been just a few years earlier. I had gone from being a Mercedes-driving millionaire with a stellar reputation as the founder and CEO of a substantial real estate business to being literally a pauper.

I had no great options to save myself and my family. Until then, pride had held me back from the only solution that could possibly work; I swallowed my pride and called my parents in China. It was the first time since I had left home fifteen years earlier that I had ever asked them for financial help. I told them that my reason for calling was that I was having "minor and temporary financial problems." I intentionally minimized the severity of my situation because I was too embarrassed to reveal the truth about my business failure and my credit card debts. I also had a lot of relatives in China who had supported me financially in coming to the States to attend Duke. I felt that I owed them all, but I could not face my shame and divulge the extent of my difficulties.

The Meaning of Resilience

The word resilience derives from the Latin verb *resilire*, which means "to jump back" or "to recoil." If you remove the prefix "re-," the root of the Latin verb is *salire*, which means "to leap." In modern English, we see the Latin origins of the word in such terms as somersault.

Being parents, however, my mother and father had an intuition about it and they read between the lines. They could tell from my voice that something was terribly wrong. Within days, they wired $30,000 to my bank account, nearly their entire retirement savings. Sometimes even the most proud and experienced entrepreneur must turn to parents, friends, or relatives for help. This is both a curse, because you have borrowed money, and a blessing, because it reinforces the pressure to succeed.

A Period of Contemplation

During the last months of 2008, I took time to reflect on all that had happened in my real estate business. I recognized that I had made mistakes and held myself responsible.

Mistake 1: Putting all my eggs in one basket. I had established my entire business in the real estate field and never imagined that the entire industry might someday collapse.

Mistake 2: Extreme shortsightedness. I was attracted to many short-term opportunities to make money, thanks to the lucrative real estate market. I was unable to look at long-term goals and build a sustainable business.

Mistake 3: No Plan B. I had no back-up plan and no strategy for managing a catastrophic failure. I had no plan for discovering new opportunities when I found myself in a crisis.

Mistake 4: False optimism and hopeful overreaching. I had over-extended my resources by buying land and properties for myself, always believing I could easily sell them for a profit.

Mistake 5: An unbalanced spreadsheet. I had accumulated too much debt and now had little cash flow.

Furthermore, there was one single overarching lesson to learn from all these mistakes. Whenever you seem to be successful and making a lot of money, you can become overconfident and believe what you do is always right. As a result, you never think that you might be doing something wrong. You never doubt yourself.

I realized I had fallen exactly into this mindset. It was time to recognize that my hubris was my Achilles' heel. I had to acknowledge that I was not perfect. I had made so many mistakes that could have been avoided, but my overconfidence had blindfolded me.

Of course, not every problem was my fault. There were strong outside forces driving the US housing bubble and leading to the total collapse of the real estate and mortgage markets. The US economy fell into what became five years of the Great Recession, the likes of which had not occurred since the Great Depression of the 1930s. I was not unique or alone; tens of thousands of businesses failed, including entrepreneurs far more successful and smarter than I.

Nevertheless, after failure, you must be willing to look at yourself and ask if you have done everything right. I had not. Being honest with myself, I learned a valuable lesson:

Any successful entrepreneur should be able to handle a market crash without getting themselves into trouble.

Smart entrepreneurs should never fail due to a crisis. They must be prepared. This insight helped me in 2020 when the COVID-19 pandemic closed down the US economy again. (In this book, I will be referring to the pandemic as simply "Covid." This crisis is discussed further in Chapter 5.) In that second crisis, I was far more prepared to weather the market hit because of what I learned after my failure in 2008.

Smart entrepreneurs should never fail due to a crisis. They must be prepared.

Discovering the Idea for My Entrepreneurship 2.0 Phase

When you encounter severe setbacks or the business you originally launched fails, but you are resilient enough to try again, you will need a new idea for your next startup venture. Where do you find new ideas?

There is a vast array of literature in the business creativity and innovation fields about how to find or formulate business venture concepts. Scores of books about entrepreneurship offer advice on techniques to generate ideas for new products or services. You may be familiar with such formal business identification techniques as incremental improvement, disruptive (radical) innovation, design thinking, blue ocean thinking, open innovation, and several other methods that have become popularized in business schools, MBA programs, and applied technology programs. If you are interested in a formal technique, you can easily find many books and online seminars to teach you.

In 2009, I had no background in any of these "ideation" techniques (and some did not even yet exist). I knew I did not want to return to the corporate world with a salaried job. I therefore had to figure out how to start a new company in some field—and certainly not in real estate. My methodology to figure out what type of new business to launch was based on a more common method accessible to any average person—study and hard work.

Ideation often arises by being able to put two ideas together, out of which you can derive or synthesize a new idea.

This form of idea creation is what happened to me. I have come to call it the "Newtonian" method of ideation, referring to the 17th-century physicist Sir Isaac Newton, who, while sitting under a tree, recognized the notion of gravity by observing the fall of an apple. While I did not sit under an apple tree, I read a lot of business news, thought about everything I read and saw on TV, and studied whether there might be a business idea hidden in the news somewhere. My "Aha!" moment came in the following four steps. I relate them all because they contain lessons that could be useful to all entrepreneurs.

STEP 1:
IDEA #1 CAN COME FROM ANYWHERE

In 2008, I had watched a TV interview program with an attorney in Los Angeles who was working in the federal government's "EB-5" program. I had never heard of this program before. EB-5 began in 1990 as a federal effort to attract foreign investment to the US to create jobs, in exchange for the investors becoming United States permanent residents after getting approval from the US Citizenship and Immigration Services (USCIS). In 2009, the program required foreign investors to invest at least $500,000 dollars in a business that would create the equivalent of 10 full-time jobs, calculated using an econometric model.

I thought my personal background could be a good match for the EB-5 program. There was an increasingly wealthy class in China looking for freedom and quality education for their children. I figured that many of them would jump into the EB-5 program. But I needed to find places to invest their money. Every EB-5 operator has to develop or find projects, such as building a hotel or apartment complex. This would not be an easy business, but I began working on identifying projects and scouting out investors. I began traveling to China, where I eventually signed many investors. But now I had to find opportunities to invest that money.

The first opportunity I found was the construction of the new international airport in Panama City, Florida. I believed it was a match for my potential Chinese investors. Funding the airport was to be a public-private partnership. I went to Panama City several times to make the contacts and learn about the project. I then began writing a proposal to submit to USCIS, which had to approve EB-5 operators to become a regional center to invest the foreign funds.

I got halfway through the proposal when I realized there were problems. A similar large infrastructure project in Philadelphia had run into a snafu and I saw the writing on the wall. The decision to accept the

EB-5 money as an investment was controlled by a board of directors consisting of many people who had no idea what the EB-5 program was about and therefore were unable to assess the risks of accepting the EB-5 capital. In Philadelphia, that board could not understand where the EB-5 money from 200 wealthy Chinese people came from and rejected that proposal. They saw this investment as "too foreign" for them. I concluded the same thing could easily happen to me and my investors wishing to invest in the proposed Florida project. The lack of control over the fund use process was fatal to this business.

I put my business plan for my EB-5 regional center on hold until the next step of the ideation process occurred.

STEP 2:
COMBINING IDEA #1 WITH IDEA #2 TO SYNTHESIZE A NEW IDEA

Late one rainy night in early 2009, I decided to read the complete 1,000+ pages of legislation—just signed by the newly inaugurated president, Barack Obama—that became known as the American Recovery and Reinvestment Act (ARRA). The goal of ARRA was to allocate federal resources that would help lift the country out of the economic malaise of the Great Recession that had started in 2008. ARRA included $120 billion in new federal spending on infrastructure projects, as well as tax relief for families in some income brackets, $100 billion in education spending, and $87 billion in healthcare expansion.

Most average businesspeople would not review the entire legalese text of a piece of federal legislation. But being as studious as I could be, I decided to read the entire ARRA verbiage to see if anything in the law might open a door to a new business idea. Why did I do this?

You never know where ideas can come from. Just read as much as you can and ask yourself, "What is there in the text I am reading that might inspire me?" Something will always pop out.

You never know where ideas can come from. Just read as much as you can and ask yourself, "What is there in the text I am reading that might inspire me?" Something will always pop out.

Sure enough, a passage in the legislation inspired me to recognize what I could do with the EB-5 investors in China whose money I could get access to. This idea arose from a section in the ARRA law that involved the Small Business Administration (SBA). In the government's efforts to spur new business development, ARRA allocated hundreds of millions of dollars that the SBA could use to facilitate a loan program targeting small businesses around the country. It was called the SBA 504 Loan Program. A small business could apply for this loan to fund the acquisition or construction of certain fixed assets, such as an office or manufacturing facility. A private lender, often a bank, must work together with a government agency called the Certified Development Company (CDC) to review and approve the application. Once approved, the business receives two separate loans—a first lien loan by the private lender and a second lien loan by the CDC. This public-private partnership program creates lots of benefits to the borrower and in the meantime helps protect the private loan.

John Shen

I wondered: *What about putting EB-5 investment capital in that first lien loan? Would that be possible?*

The "Aha!" moment hit me. As I was reading the ARRA legislation, I saw a new business model that no one else, it seemed, had thought of. I could build a private lending institution funding SBA 504 first loans to small businesses using EB-5 capital. At this point in 2009, this was such a "weird" idea that no other EB-5 operator recognized it. Combining these two federal programs—EB-5 and SBA 504—made so much sense to me because the goal of both programs was identical: job creation.

Of course, the path less traveled is not always easy. Since each of these two programs had many of their own rules, putting them together was difficult. However, you should never be afraid to create new business concepts that no one has looked at before. From there, you can ride your confidence to start an exciting journey that no one else may experience.

STEP 3:
ACT QUICKLY TO CAPITALIZE
ON YOUR IDEA

From any "Aha!" moment, the entrepreneur must move quickly—and I did! I registered a business in June 2009 to kick off my new venture. Between April and July 2009, I drafted, primarily by myself, all the key paperwork, including a comprehensive business plan, an economic report, and a full set of EB-5 offering documents, as well as other required documentation. I filed an EB-5 regional center proposal in July with USCIS. This was a critical step in the process, as I had to be approved to receive the "regional center" designation from USCIS in order to officially conduct the business.

I received a Request For Evidence (RFE) letter from USCIS in late 2009. USCIS was asking for more explanation. I had expected that, because I knew that my idea was too innovative. I took time to carefully answer over a hundred questions from the regulator and submitted my reply back to USCIS in January 2010. Then for months I heard nothing from USCIS, and my anxiety mounted. I assumed I had not been approved.

One day in April 2010, while doing some errands, I received a call from an unknown phone number. The person at the other end of the line asked me if I was a "regional center for EB-5." What? It seemed that no one had notified me that I had been accepted and approved. This person had found my phone number on the website where USCIS listed approved EB-5 regional centers. As soon as I arrived home, I jumped on the USCIS website, and yes, my regional center was listed and so was my contact information. It was one of the happiest days in my life and the start of my Entrepreneurship 2.0 phase.

But the EB-5 regional center designation took care of only one side of the business. I then worked on getting a lending license from California to become a private bank. In hindsight, I appreciated so much my decision not to file for personal bankruptcy the year before. Most people in my situation in 2009 would have probably filed a personal bankruptcy without hesitation, because that is the easiest way to wipe away all one's debts. However, if I had done that, my credit record would have been messed up and I would not have successfully received the approval to become a licensed lender in late 2010. I was fortunate that I made the right decision even though I still had to pay off over $50,000 in credit card debt in the following years to improve my credit rating.

Now I had everything to kick off a new journey.

STEP 4:
BE AGILE, FLEXIBLE, AND OPEN TO DOING ANYTHING REQUIRED

Step 4 involved a major shift in my business operations that I had to open up to. I realized that if I was going to make many trips to China to solicit investors who would be interested in obtaining permanent residency for themselves and their family members, flying out from Florida would be time-consuming. I knew that Los Angeles had a very large Chinese community and acted as a gateway for more Chinese to enter the US.

It quickly became clear that I had to move to L.A. Within one month, in May 2010, I signed a lease on an office in Long Beach, just south of Los Angeles. Because of the children, the plan was for my ex-wife and our kids to join me as soon as possible in California (and they came in 2011).

From Los Angeles, I made numerous easy trips in the following year to China. Again, acting quickly, with my rekindled confidence in being an entrepreneur, by the end of 2010, I had signed on roughly 60 wealthy investors from China who were willing to give me $500,000 each to participate in the EB-5 program. This gave me access to roughly $30 million dollars to use to co-fund small business loans with the SBA.

Lesson learned: Resilience had led me from my near-suicide in 2008 to take this further journey to a new life. My insight from reading the ARRA law in early 2009 marked the origination of what I call my "Entrepreneurship 2.0" phase. I now had a private lending company—American Lending Center—and a large supply of wealthy investors from China who eagerly sought to work with me. I felt enormously grateful that life was looking good for me once again.

Entrepreneurship 2.0

GROWING THE BUSINESS, OVERCOMING SETBACKS

Nothing comes easy when you are an entrepreneur. As with every new startup venture, I faced substantial challenges in the first years of the business. The most critical of these was that I had no experience as a private lender, let alone a lender familiar with SBA loan procedures. No one knew ALC even existed. I could not afford to do marketing to attract clients to "digest" the 30 million dollars in investor money I was sitting on. I managed to fund only a few loans to local small businesses, thanks to a friend who referred some borrowers seeking SBA loans to me.

Each of the first few loans I was able to originate was unique and in an extremely difficult situation. Failure in any one of those loans would have killed the business. However, each one was also a learning opportunity for me. The following case studies illustrate lessons that can be applied to any venture entered into by any entrepreneur.

CASE STUDY 1:
A LESSON IN PERSISTENCE, CREATIVE THINKING, AND GOAL SHARING

Among my first loans was one that involved a dentist who wanted $500,000 to expand her office in the Los Angeles area. Through the referral source, I had signed a "term sheet" with her, which was effectively a commitment to accept a loan from ALC. However, as we came closer to the closing date, she suddenly informed me that she had found another lender to fund her loan with the SBA.

The problem for me was, the investor whose money was ready to fund the loan had already filed the initial petition to the USCIS before my client changed her mind. Since the investor's daughter was at the last day before her 21st birthday (an age deadline for any kids immigrating under the parents' petition; beyond 21, young adults must apply on their own) when the petition was filed, there was no way to cancel the petition and re-file. If the investor did that, she would have lost her daughter as a dependent. We also could not change the project because the business plan submitted with the immigration petition was for the dentist's office. I had no choice but to save this deal.

Worse, I had only a little over a week left to convince the dentist to come back. At that early stage, losing a loan deal and a key investor in the meantime would easily force me to close my business.

I attempted to call the dentist numerous times, hoping to secure a chance to persuade her to return to our loan deal. She did not return any of my calls. Apparently she was determined to take the other offer. I tried to schedule a visit with her, but her office told me straight that she was too "busy" to even talk to me. I was becoming desperate because the family in China was counting on me. The clock was ticking.

Out of nowhere, a creative, though weird idea occurred to me. I would "woo" the dentist with flowers. I started sending her flowers from a different florist every day for a week, with no card to identify me as the sender. At the end of the week, I sent a final bouquet of flowers with a signed card. An hour later, the dentist's receptionist called me to thank me. I was so excited but calmly asked if I could meet the dentist for a short chat when she was available. I was told yes.

I drove to her office and met with her. I knew I had a small chance. When we sat down, I told her I appreciated the opportunity to chat and then quickly told her that the loan was not just to make a profit, but to achieve the dream of a family in China. Her eyes opened as I continued my pitch. When I stopped, she looked at me and said, "I like your perseverance." I had read her story before and knew she had a hard childhood and had sacrificed so much to become a role model of her community. So what I knew I had to say was, "I like your perseverance, too." When our two pairs of eyes connected, something clicked.

She told me that she appreciated people who work to improve the lives of others and who are persistent, as she was. Everything else was then history. We reviewed the terms of her loan and adjusted them to meet the competitor's offer. I returned to my office in Long Beach, having won a truly must-win battle. I smile every time I look at the picture we took in her office during that visit. This was not simply business. I had made a really good friend, and we still speak today.

CASE STUDY 2:
A LESSON IN STRATEGY AND CHECKMATE THINKING

This situation involved a Montessori school that was seeking a low-interest SBA loan so that it could pay off a higher interest rate loan that it already had, dating back several years. Similar to the dentist, I had signed a commitment term sheet with the owner of the school, and so we assumed the loan was ours. The investors filed the petitions with USCIS. While this was occurring, the borrower notified us that he had changed his mind and intended to sign with another lender.

Yet again, I was in a serious bind. I had already informed the families in China that their investment would be used to fund this deal. If we had to cancel and re-file the petitions, it would be a slap in my face. The school's sudden switch to another lender was unethical, having signed the term sheet. I absolutely could not afford to lose this loan.

When you have no options, you are forced to figure out how to win. You must think strategically . . . and sometimes use cunning. The solution resembles a chess game where you must make the right moves to corner your opponent's king and leave him no choice but to resign.

I knew the school was attempting to pay off a higher interest loan with the lower interest SBA loan funded with me or some other lender. After the day the borrower informed me that he was rejecting our loan, I was thinking what to do to force them to come back. By chance,

I happened to ask an experienced lender what situation would make that happen. He thought about it for a few seconds and told me a strategy: purchase the existing loan that the borrower was trying to pay off. If I did that, the borrower would have to work with me and take our loan. It was also by accident that I found the contact information of the lender of the existing loan. I then contacted that lender and offered to buy out the loan. That lender was delighted to get rid of it.

The next morning, I wired the funds to the lender and took ownership of the borrower's first loan. I then called the owner of the school and informed him that I was now the owner of his existing loan. The borrower was speechless at the moment. He had to work with my company for the new SBA loan if he wanted to pay off the first loan. If he used the other lender, I would demand control over the existing loan, which already defaulted—and then he would be stuck. Checkmate.

CASE STUDY 3:
PULLING OUT ALL THE STOPS WHEN YOU HAVE NO OPTIONS

I have found that your resilience can be bolstered whenever you believe you have no option but to survive and win. If you have nothing to fall back on, no Plan B, and no easy way out, you become driven to ensure that you end up the victor in a conflict or struggle. In my own experience, I have grown over the past decades to feel more able to take control of situations and create the right solutions. It is a feeling of owning your power.

In 2013, I faced perhaps the most substantial setback that nearly led to a complete failure of ALC and my involvement as an EB-5 regional center. By this time, I had 64 immigration petitions filed with the US government for Chinese investors seeking to invest and obtain their green cards. Their money was already invested in many SBA loans that I had found for them. Suddenly, the government decided to change the policy that determined how the jobs were supposed to be calculated in the business plan. These 64 investors no longer qualified for their green cards per the new rule.

My business was immediately paralyzed. I could not refund the 64 investors because their funds were already loaned out to US businesses. I did not have $32 million to refund each family $500,000 out of my own pocket. And even if I were able to return the money to them, my reputation as an EB-5 center would have been destroyed.

I had no options except one: *sue the US government*. I hired Ira Kurzban, one of the leading immigration lawyers in America, who wrote the law school textbook on immigration law. On my behalf, he filed a lawsuit against the US government seeking a reversal of the sudden policy change that blocked my investors. It would take over a year for the lawsuit to work its way through the court system—not what my investors in China were happy to hear.

To explain this quagmire to them, I had to travel to China and soothe every investor. For days, I had back-to-back all-day meetings, hoping I could persuade the families to wait for the courts to rule on the lawsuit. Familiar with only the Chinese judicial system, many of these families could not understand the American system, the lawsuit, or how I could possibly win against the US government. They were angry. Some suspected I was cheating them; others demanded their money back. At the end of each day, I was so exhausted and felt so defeated that I was planning to give up. But when I thought about the turn-around I was able to make back in 2008, I told myself to proceed, never give up, even for another second. I spent an entire month in China mollifying every investor, but I bought time for my attorney to work his magic.

This was darkest time in my new Entrepreneurship 2.0 phase. I was lucky that my business partners Bruce Thompson and Stella Zhang (who later became my wife) helped me a great deal. After roughly a year of incredible anxiety, the legal battle finally ended. The settlement agreements were apparently in our favor. We won. All the EB-5 investors were allowed to continue with their green card applications.

John Shen

Many of those investors ultimately became my best friends, who now regularly refer clients to me. They all received green cards and most have moved to the US and have become investors in another company I founded (which I will reveal in the next chapter).

Legal Lesson from Ira Kurzban

When I was seeking a lawyer to help me determine if I could sue the US government in 2013 when they suddenly changed the rules on the EB-5 program, I searched for the best immigration litigator in America and I was referred to Ira Kurzban, an immigration and civil rights lawyer practicing in Miami, Florida. His book *Kurzban's Immigration Law Sourcebook* has been the textbook for immigration law in every US law school, as well as the "Bible" kept in the office of every immigration law firm in the last 30 years. His knowledge of immigration law and experience practicing immigration law are the best in the country. He often represents immigrants or foreign nationals in cases against US government agencies, and even against the United Nations. His litigation record speaks for itself—he has won most of the cases, some having been extremely difficult ones. I asked Ira for his advice for entrepreneurs and this was his response:

> *If there is any lesson that entrepreneurs need to learn, it is to be open to listening to the advice that others give you.* I have worked with many people who simply do not listen to opinions from others. When people are under stress, they tend to act irrationally. What makes for a smart businessperson is being able to remain calm, listen, consider, and then make a decision. This is how you get through difficult times.

Resilience Arises When You Have No Options

To summarize what I have learned about resilience over my career, it comes down to the following principle:

> Resilience arises when you feel as if you have no options and you are committed to moving forward. When you are against the wall, you assume your power and use your wits and skill to survive.

In my experience, resilience is effectively the flip side of the same coin, with "drive" on the other side. Your drive pushes you forward towards your goals. When you hit a barrier and it blocks your drive, you use the flip side of resilience to push back.

From a psychological point of view, you need to feel and believe that you *must* go on this journey. Each time you face a minor setback, or even a major failure, your decision-making needs to be inspired and supported by this same sense, that you have no option but to take whatever steps are necessary—and work as hard as you can—to succeed.

The end result of my resilience has proven to be the cornerstone of my success. ALC avoided the complete failure I had in 2008. Fast-forward to today and ALC is now one of the most successful operators of EB-5 investments. We are still the only licensed lending institution that utilizes EB-5 money to fund SBA loans to small businesses, and there is nobody in the EB-5 arena capable of copying what we do. In the last 13 years, ALC has been the only EB-5 regional center focused on SBA loan programs and the only licensed small business lender that consistently raises

EB-5 capital to fund these loans. In the small business lending world, I have been called the "EB-5 guy" and in the EB-5 world I have been called the "SBA guy."

Resilience arises when you feel as if you have no options and you are committed to moving forward. When you are against the wall, you assume your power and use your wits and skill to survive.

ALC has offices in Beijing, Taipei, and Hong Kong (and we formerly had an office in Shanghai and Delhi, though both are closed now). We have a dual license as a California state-regulated lender and as "regional centers" approved by USCIS to support small business loans using EB-5 money. We operate 11 regional centers and many more are pending to cover most states across the country. The 2022 EB-5 Reform and Integrity Act reauthorized the program and changed many rules. Under the new rules, ALC is in a perfect position to serve thousands of EB-5 investors in the coming years.

I did all this by being driven, by capitalizing on opportunities, and by being resilient in the face of setbacks and one grand failure. In the next chapter, I will discuss how I also achieved this success by focusing on long-term goals rather than short-term gains. That is the next talent I encourage entrepreneurs to develop.

FIRST-GENERATION ENTREPRENEURS: SPECIAL ISSUES REGARDING RESILIENCE

From my experience as a first-generation entrepreneur, and from speaking with others like me, I recognize that many first-generation businesspeople struggle with resilience for a variety of reasons. First and foremost, they may feel so defeated after a complete business failure that their natural response is to give up and go home. The safety of just going home and living the life they were born into can pull on them. Returning to their native country is simpler, easier, and less stressful.

Some first-generation entrepreneurs may feel that their business failure is a sign that they cannot compete against "real" American-owned businesses. They may feel exhausted by trying to bridge the cultural gap. Or they may have faced xenophobia from customers, vendors, or neighbors—people who have treated them poorly because they are foreigners.

Above all, in my view, one of the key feelings first-generation entrepreneurs may have is that they cannot fight back against some types of situations; since they are not American by birth, they believe they hold no power. Perhaps they grew up in a culture where citizens had no rights, no freedoms, and effectively no power. Perhaps being new in America, they believe they are not entitled to own their power to overcome failure, or to fight back against an injustice. For example, how many other immigrant business owners would believe they have the power to sue the US government, as I did?

The antidote to a first-generation entrepreneur's struggle with resiliency is to remember the drive and ambition that brought you to this point. You likely overcame scores of challenges to arrive in America, to obtain higher education, to learn English, to fit into the culture, and to start your own venture. If you lost money, even if your venture failed, the determination to try again, to be better and smarter this time, may truly be the life-changing experience you were looking to find in the American Dream. If you still have the drive, you will find the resilience to succeed.

REFLECTIONS

Consider these questions. Write out your answers or identify a "success buddy" such as a business partner, another entrepreneur, or a spouse or friend with whom you can discuss the questions.

- Are you naturally a resilient individual? Are you hopeful and optimistic that things will work out well enough that you should keep moving forward and trying?

- Has your current enterprise experienced any setbacks? If so, how have you handled them? Have you persevered?

- If you are just launching a new enterprise, what steps are you taking to face and deal with setbacks? Do you have a good support network to assist you?

- Have you ever experienced a complete business failure and the need to shutter your enterprise in the past? How did you handle it?

CHAPTER 4

Long-Term Risk-Taking

RISK

- Risk: from the Italian: risco, meaning "danger," and rischiare, which means "to run into danger"

- Hazard: the chance of loss or peril

- Synonyms: danger, threat

Entrepreneurship is, in essence, all about taking risks. After all, you are using your own funds or borrowing from others to launch a venture without knowing whether it will succeed or not. The goal is to ensure your risk-taking will pay off in the end and produce profits for all stakeholders. But there is no guarantee that this result will occur. A startup is always risky, embedding danger into the opportunity.

Many entrepreneurs love the intellectual challenge and emotional thrill of risk-taking. It is indeed exciting and enticing, even addictive. For some, taking big risks bolsters a big ego. If it succeeds, the entrepreneur is a genius. If it fails, it is often dismissed as only natural when big risks are taken.

There are dozens of pithy sayings that encourage people to take risks.

- "The biggest risk is not taking any risk . . . In a world that is changing really quickly, the only strategy that is guaranteed to fail is not taking risks." —Mark Zuckerberg

- "Only those who dare to fail greatly can ever achieve greatly." —Robert F. Kennedy

- "Leap and the net will appear." —Zen saying

- "Whenever you see a successful business, someone once made a]courageous decision." —Peter Drucker

But there are very few that warn against the dangers of taking risks. Perhaps this Chinese proverb frames the warning best.

- "Biggest profits mean gravest risks." —Chinese proverb

Which do you believe?

Smarter Risk-Taking

MY VERSION OF GOING FOR THE LONG TERM

Over the course of my career, I have come to recognize that there is a right way to take risks and a wrong way. To be precise, the right approach is to always take longer-term risks, while the wrong approach is to leap at short-term gains only. Here is how I arrived at this conclusion.

When I first started my real estate venture in Florida, I was doing nothing but chasing immediate goals. I believed I could create profit "overnight." Are there a lot of opportunities like this? There are. However, what people don't seem to understand is that such super competitive opportunities are difficult to seize. If you focus only on these, it is easy to achieve nothing, even if you work extremely hard every day. We've all known people who work hard all their life but never accomplish a thing.

What is even worse is that if you are a heavy short-term planning entrepreneur, the business model you create is likely not *sustainable*. Your business becomes extremely vulnerable when market conditions change. This is exactly what happened to me in Florida. Looking back, I cannot even think of any long-term planning I did in my real estate business before 2006. What I did was primarily chase profits deal by deal, every day of the year.

After my Florida real estate businesses imploded due to the collapse of the housing bubble and economic turmoil of the 2008 Great Recession, I faced the "no options" wall. I could not return to a corporate job, as my soul yearned to start a new entrepreneurial endeavor. As I explained in the previous chapter, I reflected for months on what type of venture I could launch. It was through my propensity to do research that I happened upon the American Recovery and Reinvestment Act legislation, leading me to recognize the synergies I could create by connecting the EB-5 program and a lending practice primarily under the SBA 504 program.

EB-5 capital can be invested into many different investment vehicles at different risk levels. In the history of the program, most EB-5 investments have been made as preferred equity or mezzanine loans in the capital stack of a targeted project. These types of investments can generate higher returns, but they carry a significantly higher risk than fully underwritten senior loans. The latter, when handled properly, minimizes the investment risk, and this is why it is the most popular lending practice for banks.

The downside, however, is that when making fully underwritten senior loans, you can only charge borrowers a low interest rate and therefore you may only receive modest revenue. Essentially, my proposed EB-5 model was to create a bank-like operation and adopt the typical risk profile in banking practice. Safe? Of course. Profitable? Yes, somewhat, but it takes time.

After my colossal failure in real estate, I knew that this was not a risky project. It turned out that I did take a few years to build the necessary foundation before the business took off. But the success, though arriving a little bit "late," was never in doubt.

What really mattered, though, is that when I launched ALC, I was not seeking short-term profits, despite my financial situation still being precarious in 2010. As I was crawling out of my financial "Death Valley," making money was still important but I realized that I had to strive this time to be extraordinarily careful about taking risks. I moved deliberately and purposefully, preferring to pursue long-term goals and rewards.

From my office in Long Beach, I kicked off ALC with a couple of partners; we did every single task—from furnishing the office and opening bank accounts, to recruiting investors and negotiating with borrowers—all by ourselves. In the first year, other than a small payroll commitment, there was no operating budget. We saved our limited money to spend on traveling to China to sign up EB-5 investors. I

knew if I was not successful bringing in at least a couple of investors within a few months, we would have to stop immediately.

Compared to other EB-5 regional centers and developers, we had the skinniest budget but a big heart; big enough to build a sustainable banking business that no one had ever attempted or even probably thought about in EB-5 history. Our incredible vision and long-term growth strategies, which formed the background of our poorly funded startup, probably seemed like a joke back then. We eventually became successful primarily because of something we did correctly—I refused to focus on the short-term opportunities that would only make a quick profit.

While all this was going on, my father had been diagnosed with pancreatic cancer. While I was traveling to China, trying to find my first EB-5 investors, he was living out his last months. As he struggled to stay alive in the hospital, I remained with him for the entire night every few days. His physical condition was rapidly deteriorating that summer, and my new business was still missing its first investor. My parents had saved my life when I was down to my last $7 in early 2009. I really wanted to make this breakthrough so that I could at least share some good news with my dad before it was too late. The clock was ticking.

Long story short, I was able to sign my first investor in early August, 2010. That became one of the happiest moments in my life. I was in the hospital when I received the news from an agent for this first investor. When I got the call, I stepped away from my father's room to take it. As soon as I made sure the paperwork was completed and the deposit was in, my hand holding the cell phone suddenly started shaking. I wanted to cry and immediately rushed back to my father's bedside. A few days later, my father finally left us. I remember to this day his soft smile when I told him the great news.

Client by client, loan by loan, I grew ALC organically. Most EB-5 investors came to us through word-of-mouth referrals and personal networking with friends and business partners in China. However, with intention, I was not seeking to make millions of dollars within a few years. Instead, my dream was to build a unique business that mirrors a bank operation in many ways. I did not have any outside investors and was not interested in selling the business for quick profit either. I was focused only on transforming ALC into a long-term sustainable business.

Thinking

LONG-TERM IS SMARTER THAN SHORT-TERM THINKING

Given the success of ALC, I have settled on a single-minded philosophy to guide me about why seeking long-term rewards is smarter than chasing short-term ones. Here are three reasons to aim for long-term rewards; I recommend every entrepreneur consider these when crafting your business plan and strategy.

Less competition. If you think about it carefully, whenever there are short-term rewards to be gained, you will see many competitors vying for those same customers or that same marketplace. The common herd mentality is to be the first (even if you are not the best), the biggest, and/or to get rich quick. Let's use a class action lawsuit brought against a large corporation to illustrate this. In that scenario, the odds are against you, as one of the plaintiffs, that you would win big. You would be among millions of the company's customers who sign on to the lawsuit. If the plaintiffs' lawyers win, the court might award hundreds of millions of dollars in damages, but each "victim" receives only about $5.00. This analogy is what often happens when a market is extremely competitive and you are up against numerous other companies, everyone chasing the same short-term profits. You might end up splitting those profits into such small shares that your reward does not justify the investment you made or the risk you took.

Less potential for mistakes and bad decisions. The excitement of being an entrepreneur is often founded on taking big risks on an innovation you hope might change the world in some way.

Thousands of startups founded on new ideas launch each year, with smart, energetic, youthful visionaries eager to get their products or services into the marketplace. They move fast because they believe they do not have years of time to grow a business slowly. They may be funded by investors who themselves are pushing the venture to produce profits quickly. In my view, this is a recipe for failure. I continually see aggressive risk-taking among startups that believe they must chase the short-term profits. There is simply too great a chance for mistakes, bad planning, and hasty decision-making to occur, increasing the risk even more.

3 ***Less uncertainty.*** In my view, the key to entrepreneurship is to create a sustainable business. And sustainability requires stability and as little uncertainty as possible. Going after short-term gains is almost always full of uncertainty because, as stated above, the obvious short-term rewards are usually more competitive and more full of risks. Apparently, as my own experience showed, chasing short-term rewards does not help build a sustainable business. In contrast, going after long-term goals makes for a better business strategy. They tend to be less competitive — and sometimes you have no competitors at all. Most startup ventures do not want to wait years to bring in profit and may not even bother entering a market that you can capture for yourself. Of course, you need to have patience and enough funding and cash flow to pursue long-term goals and refrain from the temptation to veer towards the low-hanging fruit of short-term rewards. But if you can do that, and you set your sights on long-term opportunities, you will find that you can create the path to be the leading player in your industry.

I hope you take these to heart and seriously remember them when you feel tempted to go after short-term gains.

The Tortoise and the Hare

Perhaps you know the famous Aesop fable of the race between the tortoise and the hare. The tortoise walks slowly while the hare rushes so fast that he tires himself out and takes a nap, assuming he will still win. When he awakens, he discovers the tortoise made it to the finish line before him. Bummer.

We took the tortoise's approach in growing ALC, adhering to my philosophy that long-term risk-taking is smarter than getting cocky and going for short-term gains that exhaust your energy. We have grown our lending business slowly and deliberately over the past decade. We took time to study and perfect our knowledge of the government's EB-5 regulations and to develop strong relationships with the SBA and its agencies. We continuously improved our operations and client-oriented services, so our customers were highly satisfied. They rewarded

us by referring their friends and relatives, who also became clients. Our conscious focus on providing loans to women- and minority-owned small businesses proved to be timely, as both these specialized segments of SBA loans have grown extensively in the past decade.

As ALC continued to make small but steady progress, many other competitors in the EB-5 arena, including those starting late, jumped ahead of us. Some of them, in their first couple of years, made a lot more noise than us in terms of signing EB-5 investors or funding amazing projects somewhere. These were the proud hares. What happened, though, is that the majority of these hares running in the fast lane ended up with a serious legal or financial problem within a few years. While each case was different, collectively it is astonishing that almost all of them failed.

Our patience, hard work, and long-term vision paid off enormously. In March 2022, the EB-5 regional center program was re-authorized through the 2022 EB-5 Reform and Integrity Act. This update followed a few extremely "slow" years caused by the immigration visa backlogs, and the nine-months-long interruption due to Covid. Little by little, a strong EB-5 market came back in mid-2022. In this new "EB-5 2.0" era, the rules are vastly different. As most of ALC's competitors in the "EB-5 1.0" era were no longer in the game due to a variety of problems they could not solve, ALC, along with a handful of other resilient survivors, started to dominate this fast-evolving industry. In this new climate, only those who were able to work on long-term opportunities and build a sustainable business model excelled, despite being viewed as the slow tortoises before.

What I have learned over the years is simple: never fail to do long-term planning. Even though no one can predict where the market will lead in the future, establishing realistic long-term goals helps build resilience and flexibility into the products or services a business develops. To me, that is the only way to keep up with the constant evolution of any industry.

What I have learned over

the years is simple: never fail to do

long-term planning. Even though

no one can predict where

the market will lead in the future,

establishing realistic long-term goals

helps build resilience and flexibility

into the products or services

a business develops. To me, that

is the only way to keep up with the

constant evolution of any industry.

Your Commitment to Clients Is the Key to Sustainable Success

Today, ALC dominates the China market for EB-5 investors, with about four out of five prospective investors willing to choose our services. An active China market can be 75% of the entire EB-5 market; so in short, ALC is on track to become the most impactful player in the EB-5 world. Given that before 2022 we had less than 5% of the market share, our growth has been extraordinary. Why?

Our success has been based on our commitment to our clients.

From the start, our #1 goal has always been to build a solid track record in protecting our investors' interests, not chasing our own profits. In the EB-5 world, you must have an impeccable track record, avoiding mistakes or getting greedy. We have learned from our contacts in China that the majority of EB-5 regional centers or project operators have made one of three mistakes in the past:

- They have had at least one failed project that lost the entire investments of the EB-5 investors; in some cases, investors were unable to obtain the green card.

- They have had a record of some illegal operation or non-compliance caught by the US government.

- They have had some disputes with their investors, or the investor agents, that ended up with serious litigations in court.

I was told that ALC was only one of two operating EB-5 regional centers in the US that has a long history but has encountered none of these problems. This explains why the majority of investors highly trust us, despite the competition we face from other EB-5 regional centers. We stand out for having a spotless reputation protecting our investors' interests, ensuring as much as possible that they achieve their investment goals and obtain their green cards.

Starting My Second Company

ERITAGE RESORT

The story of my second startup is that it was a bit of a fluke in the context of my entrepreneurial life. I knew nothing about running a vineyard or winery in 2012 when ALC was acquiring a central Washington regional center to expand its EB-5 business to Washington State. When you operate an EB-5 regional center, you must start an EB-5 project in the authorized geographic area of the regional center within a three-year window. Otherwise, you will be forced to close the regional center. As soon as we took ownership of the regional center, we started seeking the first EB-5 opportunity in central Washington.

By chance, we found Eritage (eritageresort.com), a beautiful eight-parcel piece of land with 360 acres designated as an American Viticultural Area (AVA) located north of Walla Walla, Washington. Walla Walla Valley is a famous wine country that already featured approximately 80 wineries and 200 vineyards. Eritage was in a prime location and seemed a perfect fit for vineyard development. The previous owners had a plan to develop a winery but had not yet broken ground, as they had a serious dispute amongst themselves. The land ended up in the court for sale and I learned I could take over the property at a deeply discounted price. In hindsight, it was at best a decision with 50/50 odds; it was far from a perfect idea to own and operate this business so far from Southern California. But a good deal is a good deal, and so we submitted a bid and successfully purchased the underpriced property.

We quickly made plans to develop the land into a unique lakefront resort surrounded by beautiful vineyards. The effort took five years, but when we finally finished the work in 2017, it proved to be a boon for the entire Walla Walla wine country, as the area was immediately ranked as one of the Top Fifty Places to Visit in the World by *Travel +*

Leisure, the well-known upscale travel magazine. The news shocked the world because Walla Walla, unlike Monaco or even Yellowstone National Park, was a tiny town, unknown to world travelers. Why was it rated so high? The magazine's explanation was as simple as one word: the development of our resort Eritage. I was so proud of this accomplishment. It was an honor totally beyond our imagination.

The project was not all music, wine, and flowers. In the course of its development over the last ten years, the vineyard resort and the operation of the business have taken many twists and turns. The project helped several of my EB-5 investors who needed an investment after our lawsuits against USCIS in 2013–2014, but it was a difficult challenge for me. I lacked an experienced hospitality management team, so my team and I had to learn much about how to manage a remote project in a not-so-familiar industry.

When Covid hit in 2020, the business struggled even more. I often thought about why it was so difficult to put the project on the right track, despite the many adjustments we made over the years. I realized that the reason was that we had not done the proper long-term planning at the beginning of the project. Although it was not a complete mistake, I saw that I had jumped into an opportunistic venture triggered by a perceived short-term gain.

How could I turn this around and make it successful after many years of struggle? The answer came to me: Go back to long-term planning!

So I took time to restructure the management team in early 2021. I essentially rebuilt the team, made significant financial changes, and most importantly, spent a lot more time working on finding the right direction for the business.

Eritage is now gradually stepping out of the shadow of the pandemic, and the on-site management team is working more cohesively on the daily operation. The fundamental challenges are still there but as time goes by and the cash flow gets stabilized, everything is becoming more positive.

What did I learn from launching this business "by accident"?

When you have to roll the dice, always consider what the impact of your action could be three years, five years, or seven years down the road. If you do not have a clear vision of how to build sustainability into a new business, do not launch it, regardless of the perception of immediate gain or easily achievable short-term profit. Or, if you have already started the business without a long-term plan, sit down as soon as you can and identify your true long-term goals, and then implement the growth strategies. It is never too late to think long term.

When you have to roll the dice, always consider what the impact of your action could be three years, five years, or seven years down the road. If you do not have a clear vision of how to build sustainability into a new business, do not launch it, regardless of the perception of immediate gain or easily achievable short-term profit.

Launching My Third Company

SUNSTONE MANAGEMENT

By 2015, ALC was a clear success, thanks to the hundreds of EB-5 investors I had attracted to invest in small businesses in the US through ALC's unique investment model utilizing the SBA 504 loan program. Some of those EB-5 investors had by now begun obtaining visas to enter the US, bringing additional money with them to bank or invest. Some of them were already having their EB-5 investment paid back as well, adding to their wealth. These EB-5 clients brought in some exciting new opportunities and I was soon approached repeatedly by many of them to identify a variety of non-EB-5 investment opportunities.

I wondered if a new business might be on the horizon. The success of ALC, more specifically, the trust I had built among my EB-5 clients, perhaps offered me an opportunity to launch a new venture—a private investment company featuring private equity/credit and venture capital investments. In the same way that starting a property management company was a logical extension for a real estate agent selling homes to be used for rentals, I had a captive audience of wealthy investors eager to make further investments to grow their wealth.

I hesitated for a while. I began referring these clients to other established private equity firms and venture capitalists. But I realized that this was not working well, not because I could not make a profit out of a referral business, but because it was difficult to pass the client's trust in me to another service provider. My clients had to start from scratch to build trust with the firms I referred them to before they could decide on any new opportunities. In most cases, there was no way to make them develop that trust. When I realized this, I decided to build a new business to take care of these clients whose trust in me was already established.

In 2015, I thus launched the third venture in my Entrepreneurship 2.0 phase. I named it Sunstone Management Company. The synergies between Sunstone Management and ALC immediately formed a complementary business model. The clients for one business were directly leveraged to become clients of the other.

The business plan for Sunstone Management was quite broad—developing whatever investment opportunities might fit what our high-net-worth clients preferred. However, I needed more precision in understanding the exact needs of Sunstone's clients. Once I spoke with many of them, I learned that their number one goal was simply "parking" their money in a safe yet highly liquid place. They were looking for a higher return than what typical banks offered to their clients with a savings or CD account.

I therefore created my first private credit product—a proprietary fund featuring a fully secured investment with an annualized internal rate of return (IRR) of six percent on a one-year renewable term and without fees. This Sunstone Fixed Income Fund was the dream product that almost every new immigrant client of ALC desired. Our #1 challenge, however, was finding the right investment vehicle for the fund that would minimize our own risk. My answer came quickly: I used the SBA 504 loan program as the vehicle to invest the private credit funds raised by Sunstone. The fund had an easy start. Bingo!

Between 2015 and 2021, I upgraded the investment vehicle for the Sunstone Fixed Income Fund twice, eventually settling into some "lower middle market" opportunities offered by a key partner based in New York. The successful redevelopment of this product kept Sunstone in the fast lane of the growth race. Throughout this time, due to my conservative investment philosophy, I built an impeccable track record similar to what ALC had achieved. Up to today, the Sunstone Fixed Income Fund has not recorded any loss, neither any late payoffs nor redemptions. As a byproduct, this Fund of Funds (FOF) model made Sunstone more of a wealth management firm than a typical private equity firm.

My understanding of the clients' needs, combined with a right product, hit the target perfectly. Since its launch, Sunstone Management has grown to be as successful as ALC, especially in terms of growth rate. A large portion of the Chinese EB-5 investors who chose ALC to handle their EB-5 investments eventually joined Sunstone Management to invest and grow their wealth.

Starting in 2020, Sunstone Management has collected many awards as one of the "fastest growing companies" by prestigious media platforms. Based on its exponential revenue growth, Sunstone has been rated as one of the "Inc. 5000 Fastest Growing Private Companies in America" (and in 2020, we were on the "Inc. 500" list) as well as one of the "Fastest Growing Companies in North America" by the *Financial Times* every year so far since 2021.

The Significance of the Name "Sunstone"

The mineral known as Sunstone is a type of feldspar found in Norway, Sweden, some US regions, and on some beaches in South Australia. When viewed from certain angles, it has a spangled appearance. Sunstone is thought to be indicative of leadership. Worn as jewelry, it encourages the wearer to be open to others, benevolent, and willing to bestow blessings upon others. Also known as a stone of joy, it is believed to inspire good nature and the enjoyment of life.

In honoring this stone in our company name, Sunstone Management, we hope our business reflects leadership qualities in building a dynamic ecosystem of startups, with an abundance of energy and power, constantly inspiring people and bringing joy to our community.

John Shen

Finding New Directions for Sunstone

After a few years of crazy growth spurred by fast fund raises and massive client conversion, I saw the business was approaching a growth slowdown in creating strong net profits and meeting client demands for further development of our products and services. I believed that to properly fuel the future growth, Sunstone Management needed more long-term planning and specific long-term goals to distinguish us from other investment companies. The problem was, I thought I had already done everything I could do given my knowledge and limited time to dedicate to Sunstone Management. I did not want to compete on a short-term basis for high returns. Instead, I started to wonder how we could generate sustainability to make our business become stronger year after year.

The answer soon came to me. In the prior two decades, I had developed a strong passion to support startup companies, given my own history as a grassroots entrepreneur. Most young ventures fail not because the entrepreneurs did not work hard enough, but because it is difficult for small businesses to access the capital and resources they need to grow their business. After starting to build my own financial services one after another, I became determined to help other startups, be it with a small business loan or another form of early-stage equity investment.

I did some research to learn if I could develop a venture capital business focused on supporting startups in their early stages. I eventually found a well-kept secret in what are called "tech accelerators." These are short-term programs that provide comprehensive training and resources to qualified startups. An accelerator typically invites a small number of companies to join a "cohort" every four or six months. It invests into each of the members in the program, effectively serving as the earliest institutional investor. The goal is to help the startup grow its business, and the accelerator then shares in the long-term profit through its equity investing.

The accelerator industry was born in the early 2000s. I learned that the first group of accelerators, such as Y-Combinator (2005) and Techstars (2006), had performed extremely well in their early-stage investments, although this type of investment typically takes a long time, sometimes eight to ten years, to receive any meaningful return. As I took a closer look, I thought this investment model made sense for Sunstone. I eventually made up my mind to build a venture capital business around tech accelerator programs.

Note that investing in an accelerator program is essentially a form of long-term financial planning. If you monitor the performance of your entire portfolio, you may benefit from a few early exits here or there—for example, in a short period like two or three years—but the majority of your investment return comes in eight to twelve years from the most successful startups.

After planting many seeds in the accelerator phase, you need to stay extremely patient. Many of the early-stage investments will end up losing money or not even returning the entire principal, but these are balanced by others that will eventually pay off handsomely. Because of the amazing return rate on a typical early-stage success, sometimes hundreds of multiples, losing most deals in your portfolio does not matter much. As long as you ultimately net a great performer, often called a Unicorn (worth at least one billion dollars in valuation) at the ten-year mark, your overall investment return is still incredibly high.

The benefits of leveraging accelerator programs are huge, including:

1. Since accelerators are very competitive, they do extensive due diligence to ensure that any startup accepted has real potential to grow in the future. In fact, the claimed acceptance rate is only 2% for Y-Combinator and 1% for Techstars, much lower than even the college acceptance rate at Stanford University, the most competitive college in the US. If an early-stage investor only invests in the cohort members of an accelerator, the majority of the vetting process has already been taken care of.

John Shen

2. If you invest in the cohort members of an accelerator, you can count on the accelerating resources (mentorship, seminars, connections, services, etc.) to support the growth of the startups. Startups that do not go through an accelerator usually do not have access to such valuable resources. Having an accelerator experience can make a critical difference in this early growth stage of a company.

I decided to explore using Sunstone to invest in startups in a tech accelerator. But first I needed to find or create this accelerator.

The Creation of the Long Beach Accelerator™

By luck and coincidence, I met John Keisler, director of Economic Development in Long Beach in 2018. We initiated a conversation wherein we discovered we both wanted to launch an accelerator in the City of Long Beach. Our idea was to build a three-way public-private-education (PPE) partnership between the Long Beach city government, Sunstone, and California State University Long Beach (CSULB). We believed the three parties could work together in a new non-profit organization to operate a community-based accelerator. We immediately found our perfect partner, Dr. Wade Martin, Director of the Institute for Innovation and Entrepreneurship at CSULB, who was eager to work with us to create what became the Long Beach Accelerator.

The value and impact of our innovative PPE model cannot be over-stated. In the past, no one in the accelerator space had ever launched or operated an accelerator in the same way we were doing. No partner was strong enough to do the comprehensive work that the three of us could do collaboratively. The three parties complemented each other, and we believed that the pace of growth of our accelerator could easily be five times faster than an accelerator managed and supported only by a single private sector player.

Startup Accelerators vs. Incubators

You may have heard the terms incubator and accelerator as ways for startups to obtain mentoring and guidance. There are many differences between these two programs.

Incubators are intended to help entrepreneurs who are at the very start of the journey to validate their products and services. They come in with an idea, and perhaps a rough business plan, but have yet to start their business operation. An incubator program can last as much as a year, providing the entrepreneur with mentorship and ad hoc legal and financial advice. Incubator programs do not make connections between entrepreneurs and investors, as it is usually too premature for any investors to invest in the startups.

In contrast, accelerators are aimed at early-stage ventures that have already demonstrated a "minimum viable product" (MVP), meaning they are already in business, perhaps have some customers, and demonstrate high growth potential to produce extensive revenue and profit.

In the first quarter of 2022, I brought in John Keisler as the CEO and Managing Partner of Sunstone Management. John soon created a new vision for Sunstone, built around three pillars: Investment, Entrepreneurship, and Community. The PPE model we developed at the Long Beach Accelerator became the foundation to help Sunstone make long-term investments, promote entrepreneurship, and strengthen our community. We determined to focus on entrepreneurs—and "Founders First" became our key operating principle.

One can never overemphasize the importance of taking long-term risks in running a business. If you have not organized your business around that strategy, do it now. I did not know this at all when I started

140   John Shen

Accelerators are intensive short-term training programs, often about three months, for founders of startups, especially those in the high-tech space, where the founders receive direct guidance and instructions on how to operate their company and develop their products or services for success.

Most accelerator programs are highly competitive. A startup must submit an application for admission to an accelerator. The admission committee of the accelerator reviews all the applications and eventually decides which ones it wants to accept. When a startup is admitted into an accelerator, it becomes a member of a cohort put together by the program. Most cohort members receive an investment in either a Simple Agreement for Equity (SAFE) or a convertible note while they are in the program. When they graduate, most accelerator programs have a "demo day" to showcase these startups in front of investors and venture capital (VC) firms.

Startup accelerators can be especially valuable for companies in their very early stages, when they can benefit from the training, coaching, mentoring, and opportunities to attract investors.

The three founders (from left): John Keisler, Dr. Wade Martin, and John Shen

Eritage in 2012 and was not so clear on it yet when I launched Sunstone Management in 2015. The events of these years ultimately taught me to adopt this long-term mindset. Truth be told, it does not cure everything, but long-term planning brings the advantages of strength, flexibility, and sustainability to a business. Sooner or later, you will need these qualities to clear hurdles in your path forward.

In the following interview, John Keisler tells the story about how he, Wade Martin, and I created the Long Beach Accelerator.

John Keisler, CEO of Sunstone Management on the Creation of the Long Beach Accelerator

How did you become involved with Sunstone Management?

John Keisler

In 2015, I was the Economic Development Director for the City of Long Beach, where I had been for more than a decade. Through his company Sunstone Management, John Shen was managing money for his clients. One day he came into my office and asked me if I could help him find some technology startups in Long Beach because he was offering to have his clients invest in them. I told John that the city had just created something called the Blueprint for Economic Development, which included a recommendation to partner with a private capital investment firm to create an accelerator here in the city that would attract new technology companies to come to the city as well as help existing local technology companies continue to grow. Our meeting was synergistic, with perfect timing. We agreed to work together to fulfill both our goals.

I told John that we needed to involve an academic partner to provide the educational support and mentoring for startups. I introduced him to Dr. Wade Martin, Director of the Institute for Entrepreneurship at California State University, Long Beach (CSLB). Wade had already been operating a startup incubator associated with the university to help its business students. Shortly thereafter, the three of us agreed on a plan to create a brand new endeavor, the Long Beach Accelerator, that would help mentor and support new entrepreneurs so they would be attracted to the city to grow their companies and bring jobs to the community.

Did you organize this in a formal way, with a legal structure?

Yes. We formed a non-profit organization, a 501(c)(3), and we wrote articles of incorporation and hired an executive director to run the accelerator on behalf of a board of directors. Through Sunstone, John made a commitment to invest up to $100,000 per year and the City of Long Beach committed $25,000 per year. This money would be used to provide initial funding to the startup companies that applied to and were accepted by the Accelerator.

We then hosted a highly promoted event to launch the non-profit. We had the mayor of Long Beach, Robert Garcia, and the president of CSLB,

Jane Conoley, president of CSLB at the podium,
along with John Shen and Mayor Garcia of Long Beach

Jane Conoley, attend and we announced to the world this first-ever three-way partnership between a government, an academic institution, and a private investor to encourage entrepreneurship among students and young entrepreneurs in our community.

Who were you seeking to help with this program?

The process of becoming an entrepreneurial startup is a long journey. It takes a lot of time and money to get started. If you don't come from a wealthy family or a "friends and family" community where you might find a mentor and some financial backing, it's very difficult to get the support you need. There's no surrounding culture for entrepreneurship for many young immigrants, women, and people of color. These are usually under-represented entrepreneurs — and they need assistance. Reaching out to this audience was very consistent with our values in Long Beach and also at CSLB, which is a publicly funded state university whose mission is to provide access to education for all and to create economic opportunity. So our mission resonated for all three parties. Let me quote you from the Accelerator's website (www.lbaccelerator.org) to summarize who we seek to help, because not only are we helping entrepreneurs, but we sought to help the city too.

> The Long Beach Accelerator mission is to accelerate early-stage startups with mentoring, seed funding, and an exit strategy. We are also committed to one unwavering principle — that you can do it all with the support of the City of Long Beach, a community from which you can recruit top talent and also call your home. Along with a business-friendly environment, Long Beach offers a place where employees can live, work, and play.

When did the Accelerator formally launch?

We launched it formally in 2019, though due to Covid, the first cohort did not start until 2021. By the beginning of 2023, we will have graduated four cohorts. In this time, we have attracted 40 new technology companies from the city or outside of the city to seek our help in supporting them as they grow and work towards becoming truly successful, sustainable businesses.

How does the Accelerator work?

Twice per year, we open up the program to a cohort of about ten young entrepreneurs who are at the beginning stages of having an existing business operating in the world. They must have a product, a market, and some profit when they apply. The application process is highly competitive, with only about 1 in every 100 applicants accepted. Those who are accepted are aligned with mentors to help them better structure their business to scale and grow it, and most importantly, to appeal to the venture capital investors that Sunstone Management will introduce them to at the end of the program, which is about four months later.

What happens then? Do you invest in them at this point?

One of the advantages of joining the Accelerator is that we help each company build its valuation, which is needed to attract investors. When they enter the program, they are valued usually at around $1.5 million, given their technology and customer base. This is a rather standard valuation for early-stage companies. Sunstone Management then invests from $100,000 to $200,000 in each of the companies in the cohort, which amounts to about $1 million in total that we put in. This is money that Sunstone obtains from our clients who invest in mutual funds we have created focused on early-stage startup ventures. In exchange, Sunstone gets roughly a 6% stake in the company's equity, though this is just a general rule and can differ from company to company, negotiated on an individual basis. The startup then uses a portion of that money to pay the Accelerator program for the training and mentoring they will receive. (Remember that the Long Beach Accelerator is a non-profit so it needs some operating capital, too.) By the way, this is considered pre-seed capital, which is not the same as angel money, which comes in at a later stage.

SUNSTONE
University

What training do these entrepreneurs get in the Accelerator and who mentors them?

Every startup founder needs help and support. That is what the program is aimed at providing. For four to six months, the founders take classes and have access to technical training through CSLB, as well as personal mentoring and coaching. The founders also have access to all the cohorts in the group, which forms a tight network of support and collegial advice from their peers.

One of the most significant benefits of the program is that the companies get access to members of Sunstone's executive team or to people in our network who have expertise in their business sector. These people serve as their mentors, and some even join the startup's board of directors to provide ongoing assistance and guidance. So, overall, the entrepreneurial founders really benefit because we connect them with resources in their specific sector who help them really refine and grow their business.

What happens at the end of the Accelerator Program?

One key thing that happens at the finish of the program is that we reappraise them with a new valuation. If they were valued at the start of the program at, say, $1 million and now we've seen growth and improvement in their business plan, a better product, and improved market fit, we might assign them a value of $3 to $5 million. This greatly aids their ability to attract investors. Sunstone Management might even invest more at this point, perhaps another $400,000 to $800,000. Next comes the exciting part. We have what's called a "Demo Day" where the startups have an opportunity to present their company and pitch to angel investors who come to watch and listen. Those investors might invest another $50,000 or $100,000 right on the spot, or we might have an angel syndicate composed of many investors attend, and they might invest upwards of $250,000 in exchange for a share of equity. This is still early-stage investing, but any amount the startup gets helps.

Does the Accelerator Program end after the Demo Day?

We encourage the top prospects to remain in the Accelerator. Some have stayed for another six months or even a year to continue developing their business with our assistance, education, and mentoring. This can be critical to prevent early-stage failure, which is common for many startups that begin faltering within their first two years. It's really sort of like insurance for our investors to make sure the startups gain the skills, knowledge, and support they need to be successful and pay our investors back.

For the companies that stay, Sunstone Management even offers to help them with a new round of investing. After the Demo Day, they may have as much as $1 million to $1.5 million in cash to work with, but they now need more. For this, we actually use EB-5 money through ALC, because the startup can now qualify as a small business. This means, however, that it must create at least 10 jobs for every $800,000 investment using EB-5 investor money. We believe we can really help them find workforce development support or we can offer them a shared human resources director, whatever it takes to grow them to the next phase of their development. Our goal is to ensure they are successful, as it is a win-win for them and Sunstone Management, as well as for the City of Long Beach.

Have you had any successes so far?

Yes, we have had several companies obtain substantial financing to the tune of about $12 million from angel investors as well as from VC firms. Four firms have been acquired, but it is too early now for most of the cohort members to be mature enough to be acquired for large multiples of their valuations.

Does your Accelerator have any competitors?

Yes, there are several out there. Some other cities have created startup incubators or accelerators, or have hosted them, or become partners with them, and maybe even use some of their government funds to help them operate. But our Accelerator is unique in being a partnership between a private venture capital firm working with a local government and an educational institution to actually form a non-profit, with all of us sitting on the board. Plus it is unique for a venture capital firm such as Sunstone to actually raise capital for each of the cohorts in the Accelerator and to make a commitment to support them as Sunstone does. I don't know anybody who's put all three together and then incorporated them into a non-profit entity, as well as helping fund each accelerator startup, and even sitting on their boards and raising capital for each cohort. This makes what we do unique.

What we do is also very different from the usual venture capital company that passively invests in startups by just writing a check and then remaining hands-off in the background. Our strategy is to embed some of our executive team leaders from Sunstone Management or from our contacts right into the board of each winning team to assist them in securing successful implementation and growth. So far, we have seen several teams benefit greatly from this hands-on philosophy of venture capital funding.

Finally, let me also repeat that this partnership is also unique in that our mission is to help the underrepresented entrepreneurial class—women and minorities—get their start in entrepreneurship. We aim to provide access and training to this sector, something that few venture capital companies do.

What is your view of entrepreneurship in America?

My philosophy about all this begins first and foremost with the role that entrepreneurship plays in the American economy. We have a capitalistic economy that rewards people who capitalize on opportunities they want to exploit. They can retain ownership of their ideas and the solutions they create, and this creates tremendous incentives for entrepreneurs. We also have these incredible educational institutions where people from all over the world come to learn. Our society is one that embraces diversity and openness to immigration. These creative people can move around within our economy and within our country and they can find the educational resources and capital they need.

Finally, we also have a large sector of investors, people who are willing to take a bet to invest money in this entrepreneurial economy. America as a nation represents over 51% of the venture capital activity world-wide. California alone is the biggest powerhouse of investment. There's a density of venture capital in this state that exceeds anywhere else in the nation. New York and Massachusetts are right behind, but by a wide margin. So it's a really incredible environment in California for entrepreneurs. I don't think that what we're doing at Sunstone Management can be done anywhere else in the world.

As for entrepreneurs in America, these are the people who see opportunity to solve a problem and then capitalize on that solution for the purpose of making money or gaining a private benefit. That's what keeps them motivated. They're usually very creative people who are connected to the world with great curiosity. They not only love finding problems, but they're confident they can find solutions.

To truly be an entrepreneur, you have to not only have the idea for a solution to a problem, you have to have the hardcore skillset to implement it. And so it takes curiosity, awareness, and skills to pull the resources together to actually do it. It's all stitched together with persistence and hard work.

Sunstone Management fits in here because we know it's really difficult and founders can't do it alone. They need support and resources; whether it be insight, technical assistance, or the capital resources to actually make it happen. So this is a very special mission that I believe we are fulfilling.

Do you enjoy your work?

I was an economic development director for many years and worked in the City of Long Beach for over 17 years. As CEO of Sunstone Management, I'm effectively doing a lot of the same work and working in the same world, trying to make a difference in helping small businesses and grow jobs in our communities. But this job extends beyond that, as we are working now with the Cal State and UC universities all across California, as well as in New York. This is much more expansive. But most of all, I enjoy working with John Shen. He is a remarkable person and a real visionary for us all.

Falling into "Parallel Entrepreneurship"

Back in 2010, I had no idea what I would achieve with ALC, nor that I would eventually be launching and operating three companies by 2015 in what I would eventually come to call my Entrepreneurship 2.0 phase.

To a large extent, I slipped into being a parallel entrepreneur without realizing it. For each company I launched, I was able to minimize the hardship and pain that a solo entrepreneur normally experiences. A key reason was that I was able to build a small but powerful leadership team that helped me manage the daily operations with exceptional ease. Eritage was the most difficult situation, however. The management company we had hired at the outset laid the foundation for the resort development, but I eventually decided to hire our own manager in 2020, which put the business on the right track for profitability.

Launching Sunstone Management was the point at which I realized I was truly becoming a parallel entrepreneur. It felt like starting a new and exciting business all over again, in that it required the majority of my time and focus. Without employees, I accepted that I had to do all the initial work to launch the company myself. I was confident that I was on the right journey, despite the hard work. As the business was looking for new opportunities to get to the next level, I made a critical decision to hire a new CEO and adjust the vision of the business. When the dust settled, Sunstone Management became a much stronger and healthier business.

In the next chapter, I will show how you can use your first company to find new businesses to launch and why becoming a parallel entrepreneur makes more sense than remaining a solo or a serial one.

FIRST-GENERATION ENTREPRENEURS: SPECIAL ISSUES REGARDING RISK-TAKING

As a first-generation immigrant in America who has taken short-term risks and lost it all—and who has taken smarter long-term risks and done exceptionally well—I can speak to the feelings that drive first-generation entrepreneurs. When you are new to the US, the American Dream is a powerful force. With America's entrepreneurial capitalist system, alluring freedom, and flashy wealth, it is tempting to believe that the American Dream can be yours within a short time if you work hard enough. Especially if you came here as a student, as I did, you feel that your American diploma is your ticket to riches and happiness. You might be driven to be entrepreneurial, in fact, because it appears to be the fastest path to this Dream, rather than spending thirty or forty years working for a company.

However, I suggest that the drive to attain this American Dream can mislead first-generation immigrants to opt for short-term rewards over long-term sustainability. Immigrants often feel an unbearable pressure to succeed so they can become a "real American," not just "an immigrant like so many others." There is a feeling that we must show the world we are as good as any natural-born US citizen, that we are as smart as them. And so we become shortsighted, believing that we can launch a business, work constantly and hard, and soon we will be happy and wealthy.

As you have read in this chapter, I would recommend that you refrain from chasing short-term rewards. Yes, the promise of wealth may appear to be worth the hard work, but what you risk is often greater than the potential rewards. As much as possible, take time to examine the long-term goals you can achieve with your venture rather than choosing a quick path to wealth. I believe you will build a stronger, more robust and sustainable business if you plan for the longer-term future than for just the next few years.

REFLECTIONS

Consider these questions. Write out your answers or identify a "success buddy" such as a business partner, another entrepreneur, or a spouse or friend with whom you can discuss the questions.

- Are you a risk-taker? What is an example of a risk you have taken in the past?

- Have you ever decided not to take a risk on a short-term bet in favor of a long-term opportunity?

- In your venture, what are the short-term rewards you could target? What are the longer-term rewards? Might you be better off if you forsake the short-term ones for the longer-term ones?

- Do you have the finances and time to stay in business in order to target long-term goals rather than short-term rewards?

- List some reasons that you cannot delay rewards and must go for short-term results? Then list the counterpoint arguments as to why you might be better off giving up on those short-term results and opting for long-term planning.

CHAPTER 5

Strategic Thinking

STRATEGY

- From the Greek *strategia*, meaning "office of a general"

- To lead, take command, make a plan of action

- Synonyms: tactic, scheme, policy

156   John Shen

In 2017, I entered what I now refer to as my Entrepreneurship 3.0 phase. This was when I launched yet another company, which made me acknowledge that I had gone beyond being a "solo entrepreneur" and was *truly* becoming a "parallel entrepreneur."

Needless to say, being a parallel entrepreneur is far more difficult and strenuous than being a solo or serial entrepreneur. Why would an entrepreneur want this additional challenge, responsibility, and stress? My answer:

> There are significant business-enhancing benefits to be gained by owning and operating multiple businesses simultaneously. And it is not as hard to accomplish as you may think! You can actually have fun!

I believe that any driven, ambitious entrepreneur with one business already operating successfully can (and should) entertain pursuing parallel entrepreneurship. It provides more fun, excitement, and potential payoffs than being a solo or serial entrepreneur. When you simultaneously run multiple companies, you experience more intellectual stimulation and emotional highs than operating just one firm at a time.

Strategic Thinking

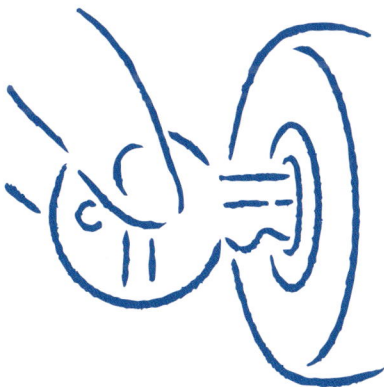

THE KEY TO GOING PARALLEL

Being a parallel entrepreneur requires a high level of drive, the ability to capitalize on opportunities, resilience, and the mindset of long-term risk-taking—all talents covered so far in this book. But you can't stop there.

I believe that any driven, ambitious entrepreneur with one business already operating successfully can (and should) entertain pursuing parallel entrepreneurship.

It provides more fun, excitement, and potential payoffs than being a solo or serial entrepreneur.

When you simultaneously run multiple companies, you experience more intellectual stimulation and emotional highs than operating just one firm at a time.

To grow into being a successful parallel entrepreneur, the next key talent you need is *strategic thinking*. What does this mean? In Chapter 2, we discussed the importance of being able to capitalize on opportunities you spot among new trends in the marketplace. Strategic thinking is related to that attribute, but strategic thinking goes much deeper, as it helps you actually create your own new opportunities.

When I use the term *strategic thinking*, I am referring to three very specific skills:

Leveraging and Mutual Leveraging. When you seek to operate multiple businesses, there is a potential enormous benefit: leveraging shared opportunities. The product or service in one business can lead directly to a new product or service in your next business. Likewise, the client base for one business can often become the exact same client base for another business. Moreover, there could be opportunities that make businesses complement each other and feed off each other. That way, instead of having one business help another, you grow both by letting them help each other. I call that "mutual leveraging." I will show you how I've been able to both leverage and mutually leverage my businesses with real examples.

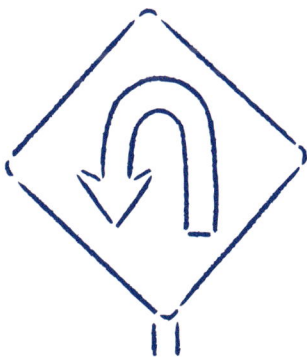

Pivoting. Sometimes things do not go the way you thought they would. When this occurs, you cannot be caught like a deer in the headlights. You need to take action and change course, often referred to as pivoting. The goal is to be agile, strategically, meaning you are able to quickly figure out how to move in a different direction to avoid revenue loss and possibly failure.

Innovating. Owning multiple businesses also enlarges your perception of market demand in different sectors. With this wider view, you are often able to innovate new products or services. I will demonstrate how I have brought innovation into every one of my businesses as a way to expand revenues in those companies.

Let's take a look at each of these strategies.

The 1st Type of Strategic Thinking

LEVERAGING AND MUTUAL LEVERAGING

In many ways, the foundation of all my successes has been leveraging. It began in 2010, when I recognized that I could leverage money from wealthy Chinese investors interested in the federal government's EB-5 program as the foundation of launching my private lending institution, ALC. Next, when I launched Sunstone Management, the idea for this occurred because I realized that many of my EB-5 clients who had invested in small business loans with ALC now wanted to find new investment opportunities in non-EB-5 projects. Sunstone Management was born directly out of tapping into the existing client base of ALC. I was effectively monetizing the same roster of clients twice.

I have used this strategy repeatedly to grow my businesses, especially as I started operating more companies. When leveraging happens, two or more of my businesses simultaneously benefit from the collaborative efforts. To me, mutual leveraging is the most efficient way to grow multiple businesses. It is so much fun! This unique excitement never hits solo or serial entrepreneurs. Here are some examples.

To me, mutual leveraging is the most efficient way to grow multiple businesses. It is so much fun! This unique excitement never hits solo or serial entrepreneurs.

LEVERAGING AND MUTUAL LEVERAGING BETWEEN ALC AND SUNSTONE

When Sunstone Management first launched, my goal was to help ALC clients manage and grow their wealth. Initially, the company was primarily designed to be a private boutique investment firm. To start, I invested Sunstone clients' money in those SBA loan projects I was developing for ALC, through a proprietary fund called Sunstone Fixed Income Fund. However, I immediately realized that the profit margin of those loan investments, without financial leverage, was not high enough to cover a fixed return rate of 6% plus extra net profit for the Sunstone Fixed Income Fund. Essentially, Sunstone Management was competing against banks in China that offered many similar products. Given that US-based investment firms and banks did not sell similar products, it was difficult to find the right underlying investment structure to meet the required needs of the Sunstone Fund.

As I was scratching my head, my small business lending knowledge kicked in. I realized that I could probably find opportunities in US lower-middle market funds, quite similar to the small business market. This led me to form a partnership with an exceptional fund management firm headquartered in New York. In the end, I was able to select a few private credit/equity products targeting the US lower-middle market in the portfolio of that fund manager as the investment vehicle I could tap into for the Sunstone Fixed Income Fund. If I had not understood the demand and available investment products for US small businesses, I would not have been able to create this solution.

A short while later, I saw that many of my Sunstone clients were interested in venture capital investments, so I started looking for equity investment opportunities. My background in funding small businesses quickly led me to think about early-stage startups. To learn about this type of investing, I decided to become an angel investor myself. I joined a nationwide angel investment group, the Seraph Group, in 2014. This helped me learn how to invest in such opportunities as a professional fund manager. I developed a strong partnership with Tuff Yen, founder of Seraph Group. By the time Sunstone formed its first venture capital fund, I already had an exceptional mentor and a good sense of how to navigate through the complicated VC investment world. I effectively leveraged my personal experience and resources as an angel investor to develop the VC investment opportunities for Sunstone.

As I became experienced and successful raising funds for early-stage investments, I met John Keisler and Wade Martin, Director of the Institute for Innovation and Entrepreneurship (IIE) at California State University Long Beach (CSULB). As I recounted in the prior chapter, the three of us clicked immediately in deciding to collaborate in a public-private-education partnership that became the Long Beach Accelerator. Since its launch in 2019, this accelerator has expanded rapidly, thanks to the investment expertise that has become the trademark of Sunstone Management in the startup community. Today, when accelerators look for investment partners, they know Sunstone is always one of the best options.

Another fast-growing leveraging opportunity for Sunstone Management in the last few years has been building partnerships with universities that teach innovation and entrepreneurship. This idea first came about when I met with Professor Wade Martin in 2018 to discuss what Sunstone could do to support the entrepreneurial activities on his campus. He told me that he was already running what he called the Innovation Challenge, an annual business plan (pitch) competition for the CSULB students, faculty, and staff. On the spot, I made an immediate decision to offer that Sunstone Management would sponsor his event, giving award funds to the winning teams. The offer was accepted.

In our honor, the event was renamed the Sunstone Innovation Challenge and has grown steadily every year since then. That sponsorship then opened the door for Sunstone to build long-term partnerships with many other universities and colleges, all to support the growth of the startup communities. This proved to be invaluable in connecting Sunstone with many early-stage businesses offering exciting investment opportunities.

Even better, one day a year later, I was having breakfast with Wade and I asked him about his ultimate dream for our future collaboration plans. The success of the Sunstone Innovation Challenge apparently boosted his sense that we should replicate it elsewhere. We decided to take another giant step in building something bigger. This was to be two events: the first-ever cross-campus startup pitch competition, and a cross-campus demo day open to the entire California State University (CSU) system, the largest public university system in the US. Wade and IIE took on the responsibility of organizing and hosting the two events, and Sunstone made a multi-year financial commitment to sponsor them.

The two unprecedented events, the CSU Sunstone Startup Launch (the pitch competition) and the CSU Demo Day, both powered by Sunstone, debuted in 2022 on the CSU Long Beach campus, with several dozen teams of entrepreneurs pitching and young startups

demoing their ventures. While the first Sunstone Innovation Challenge was a form of leveraging the personal trust between Wade and myself, the CSU cross-campus events represent an example of how the two of us leveraged the previous successful experience of the Sunstone Innovation Challenge to create what has become one of the most impactful annual shows in the California startup ecosystem.

Here are two more examples of how I have leveraged ALC and Sunstone. First, in May 2020, the EB-5 market came back strong when a revised EB-5 law became effective. Meanwhile, ALC had changed its funding strategies to take advantage of the government's desire to award a large share of visas to EB-5 investors who invested in "rural projects." As an owner and key management team member for both companies, I realized that the EB-5 capital ALC raised could be a perfect funding source for rural opportunities developed by Sunstone. In fact, this new government focus, by coincidence, was well aligned with Sunstone's new business priority to build rural innovative startup ecosystems. It made perfect sense to push the two complementing businesses to work even more closely to seize the unprecedented opportunities in funding rural EB-5 projects. This time, again, ALC's EB-5 investors and Sunstone's startup ecosystem won big as both companies benefitted from the mutual leveraging.

Second, in late 2022, ALC became a State Small Business Credit Initiative (SSBCI) lender in California. The main targeted borrower group of this program is startups. This accreditation allowed us to yet again create another leveraging opportunity. Given that Sunstone invested into many California startups through accelerators and other sourcing platforms, it could now easily provide ALC access to a large and high-quality pool of prospective borrowers—startups seeking business loans to supplement or complement investments they received (or did not manage to get).

In effect, through leveraging and mutual leveraging, both ALC and Sunstone Management are monetizing our client bases several times to fund targeted opportunities, and then leveraging those investments to create profits. Leveraging and mutual leveraging create a virtual spiral that keeps fueling the growth of both companies.

Leveraging, as a general growth strategy, can help any single business. But as a parallel entrepreneur running many growing businesses, you have the best opportunity to develop synergy among your businesses through mutual leveraging. Mutual leveraging does not take an existing product, service, or current clients of one business and give to another business. Instead, it boosts the business development of two or more businesses simultaneously. The end result? All the involved businesses grow by growing their products, services, and/or client base.

Leveraging is like a foot race where one runner hands the baton over to the next runner. A parallel entrepreneur uses leveraging to win the race!

John Shen

Here are four of the many ways Sunstone and ALC are leveraging each other to create an amazing cycle of self-sustaining wealth creation and an entrepreneurial success model.

1. Sunstone Management creates funds that its clients can choose to invest in, dedicated solely to providing seed capital to startups in the accelerator programs including the Long Beach Accelerator.

2. The startups may receive equity investments from angel investors and/or VC companies that improve their valuations and opportunities to grow.

3. The top startups may also receive additional funding from investors in the EB-5 program through a variety of unique loan programs by ALC. This now creates the majority of profits for ALC.

4. Sunstone Management and ALC clients, in different ways, both have opportunities to benefit when any of the startups in which they invested achieve financial success.

Interview with Wade Martin and John Keisler regarding University Partnerships

Wade Martin and John Keisler provide their thoughts on developing the Sunstone Innovation Challenge and then expanding it to include the entire California State University system plus other universities.

Wade, how did you become involved with Sunstone Management?

I have been the Director of the Cal State Long Beach Institute for Innovation and Entrepreneurship, which is an independent institute on campus that provides extracurricular education and support for students interested in entrepreneurship. For years, we were hosting a pitch competition for students. The process would begin in the fall semester where student teams would start to learn about entrepreneurship and begin ideating a business concept. We would encourage students to work in teams composed of people with different skill sets. The students could be majoring in anything, be it liberal arts, business, or engineering. By spring, they would have learned about creating a business plan. At the end of that semester, the teams would then present their business idea and plan and a panel of judges would select four winners: 1st and 2nd places, and two honorable mentions. Each winner would receive a small amount of prize money.

When John Shen and I met, he was immediately interested in our competition and offered to fund the prize money for the awards for three years, starting in 2019. The university administration agreed to rename the pitch competition the Sunstone Innovation Challenge. We have had some very interesting winning teams; for instance, a team that developed a new process for night vision goggles, a team with a new communications platform for learning management, and a team that invented a 3-D printed violin to lower the cost of violins for young music students.

What are the two new events you are hosting?

Recently, John Shen, John Keisler in his role as CEO of Sunstone Management, and I worked together to expand the original pitch competition to two new events.

The first is the CSU Startup Launch, which is a pitch competition we are now opening to students at all 23 of the Cal State campuses. This will be a competition where students compete at their individual university branch, and then those winners will compete in a final pitch competition here at CSLB. We held the first one in May 2022, which was open to six Cal State campuses, and in 2023 it will be open to all 23 campuses.

The second event, called the CSU Demo Day, commenced in October 2022 and is a demo day competition open to students, faculty, and alumni teams from the entire CSU system. Participants include early-stage businesses that are already up and running but need feedback and funding. They compete in a TV-show *Shark Tank*-style presentation in front of actual investors who may be willing to invest in their venture. Our goal is to demonstrate that the Cal State University system is full of entrepreneurs who can lead the world in new ideas and businesses.

What is the incubator that you are developing?

We now have a goal to provide a clear path for anyone in the CSULB system who is interested in entrepreneurship. As students, they can take the business courses we offer relative to entrepreneurship, both in the undergraduate and graduate programs. Next, we are working on creating an incubator, which will provide very early, first-stage training and mentoring for students who want to start a business. Those whose ideas are worth pursuing can then apply to the Long Beach Accelerator for more focused and deep support, mentoring, and opportunities to attract investors.

The next set of questions was directed at John Keisler, CEO of Sunstone Management.

John, what is your vision for these pitch and demo days that you are having Sunstone Management support?

In expanding the Sunstone Innovation Challenge to include all 23 Cal State campuses and 10 University of California campuses throughout California, our goal is to attract the top talents from this enormous system of superior educational institutions in the US. The events potentially invite about 550,000 students, faculty, and alumni in the Cal State system and another 200,000 students, faculty, and alumni in the UC system to learn about the startup pitch days, the Demo Days, and the Long Beach Accelerator.

Many of these schools, especially those among the UCs, like UC Berkeley, are ranked among the top 20 universities in the entire world. There's a huge amount of talent on these campuses, young people who might one day start their own entrepreneurial ventures. These schools are all publicly funded, and they have huge resources to help students obtain grants for research and development, new technology innovations, and intellectual property creation. This is a massive potential audience to attract into entrepreneurship in California. It's an incredible opportunity to tap into an enormous talent pool and not only introduce them to entrepreneurship, but also to Sunstone Management, which might one day be able to help them get started in their venture with our investments and mentoring. We want to get to know these students at the very beginning of their entrepreneurial thought process and encourage them to become part of our family. This approach fits right into our business model—to create the largest community of early-stage entrepreneurs that we can someday invest in and profit from.

Leveraging

HOW I STARTED MY 4TH COMPANY

My next company was also created based on leveraging.

Over the years, many of my clients at ALC and Sunstone Management had requested me to serve as the trustee of their US-based trusts because of my acquaintance and a strong personal trust. While I was honored to fulfill this role of being the trustee, taking on its responsibilities is a legal obligation with very precise and professional standards. The trustee must perform as a professional fiduciary to ensure that the terms of the trust agreement are carried out correctly, so the position requires extremely deep financial, legal, tax, and other training, especially when a large amount of assets are placed in the trust. I was simply not qualified. But as I tried to look for a professional trustee for my clients, it turned out to be too difficult, mainly due to the language and cultural barrier. In California, unfortunately, there are not many licensed trustees that can handle the needs of first-generation immigrant Chinese families.

What Is a Trust Company?

Setting up a trust is quite a popular endeavor among wealthy families, globally. A trust is established to primarily help the grantor transfer assets to their designated beneficiaries. Depending on the type of trust created, an established trust structure can receive tax, legal, and asset management benefits. To properly execute a trust agreement, the grantor must assign someone, either a natural person or a licensed financial institution (corporate/institutional) as the trustee to do the work. The trustee thus takes on significant fiduciary responsibilities.

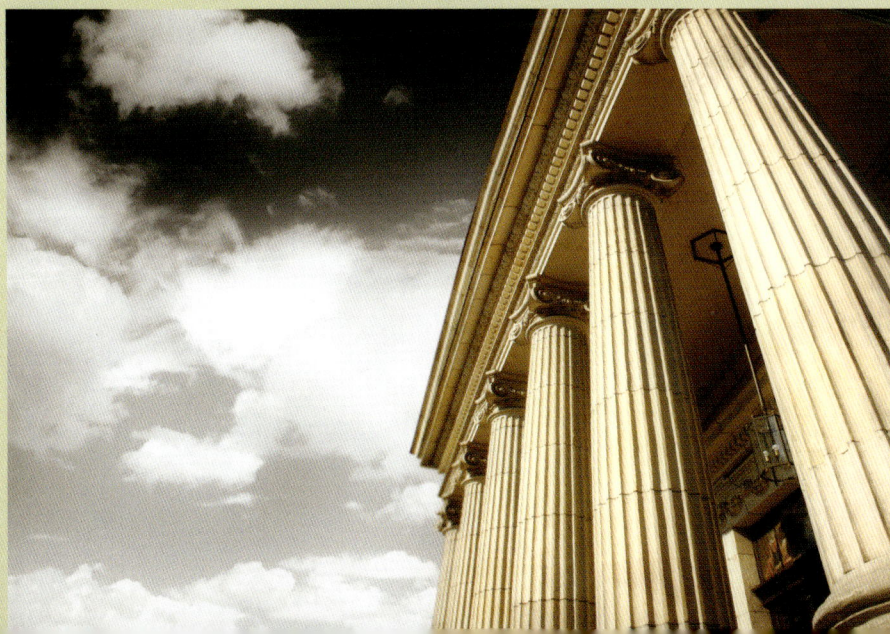

Given that my name was eventually put on a few trust agreements by my clients, I was forced to think of long-term solutions. I did some research and spoke with many professionals who had a strong understanding of the trust business. What I saw was an incredible niche market for corporate trustee service providers who could build and maintain a high level of confidence with many high-net-worth new immigrant families. I thought, why not launch a licensed trust company?

Starting a new trust company, however, required jumping a huge hurdle. I would need to obtain a California chartered license under the Trust Law. Because of the substantial fiduciary duty a trust company carries, the licensing requirements in California are extremely stringent, and the application process itself could easily take two years. No wonder there were only seven active licensed independent trust companies in California. The most recent California trust license was issued more than 15 years ago. Moreover, I also realized that the existing operating trust companies, like highly regulated banks, were under close scrutiny by the regulators. Could I handle this work, and if so, where should I start?

I hired a well-known law firm specializing in financial licensing services to help file the trust license application. Daniel Wheeler, who had extensive experience in handling compliance work in the financial industry, was the lead attorney for this project. I needed his guidance to help us navigate through this enigmatic process. He left the law firm halfway through the process but agreed to stay on the team and help us complete the application.

During a phone conversation one day about the future of this business, we shared our business visions of the new company. Since he had spent so much time working on our trust license application, Dan had come to understand my strengths and weaknesses as the company's leader. His background and experience fit right into being part of a highly regulated financial service business. I did not have anyone else in my network who could handle this critical aspect of the trust company. I thought perhaps Dan might want to be an entrepreneur working with us.

The decision gelled in my mind and I soon invited Dan to become the CEO of the new organization—Sunstone Trust Company. Since then, he has done a superior job. Sunstone Trust Company finally received its California trust license approval in April 2021. The company then became fully operational that summer.

This business concept was built on the demand of many clients of my other businesses, ALC and Sunstone Management. It was yet again an example of leveraging opportunities that parallel entrepreneurs can have once they've built a portfolio of multiple successful businesses. In the approved business plan of Sunstone Trust Company, we were targeting a highly underserved market with low-hanging fruit. When the operation started, we literally were able to go straight to "onboarding" clients rather than prospecting for them. We immediately had a huge audience of wealthy families who had strong confidence in ALC, Sunstone Management, or me personally. If they had the need for the service, they had zero hesitation to become a client of Sunstone Trust Company.

Many Other Ways to Leverage

Leveraging is so vital to my business success that I literally spend time as often as I can to do strategic thinking, seeking how I might develop new ideas on how to leverage one of the businesses or its clients, its methods, or processes. I especially look for synergies among my three financial-industry businesses—ALC, Sunstone Management, and Sunstone Trust Company. I believe that when you have multiple businesses, with all of them growing in revenues and size, you can discover

Leveraging is so vital to

my business success that I literally

spend time as often as I can

to do strategic thinking,

seeking how I might develop new

ideas on how to leverage one

of the businesses or its clients,

its methods, or processes.

myriad opportunities to double, triple, even quadruple dip into your client base. You can cross-sell anything if you have overlapping businesses. Compared to finding and developing a brand new market for a business, leveraging one's clients is a much more efficient process to expand your products and services and increase revenues and profits.

Here are five methods that I can generalize about how to leverage:

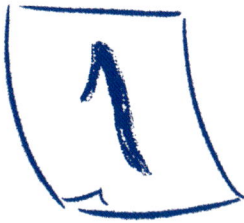

Leverage the client base. If you look hard enough, you can sometimes find a way to tap into your existing client base to sell them a new product or service through a surprisingly easy maneuver. One time recently, for instance, I discovered that I could offer Sunstone Management's clients a new service by simply filing some paperwork. I didn't need to hire new staff or spend money on marketing. After signing an application, I could easily take advantage of leveraging the resources of one current business to create a new financial service for its existing clients.

Leverage the staff and/or executive leadership team. ALC constantly onboards new EB-5 investors. When I started Sunstone Management, I used the same staff to onboard new clients to invest into non-EB-5 opportunities. Since many ALC clients became Sunstone Management clients, it made the work easy and smooth for my staff, who were familiar with most of these existing ALC clients. When Sunstone Trust Company started later, some of the staff joined the new company. Their main project was to bring the clients of ALC and Sunstone Management over to Sunstone Trust Company. While the service might look different to these prospective trust clients, the face of the staff or trust in them did not change. The same thing occurred for the leadership team.

The executives on the first business can always work part-time to help subsequently launched new businesses in the first six months or year. Since it always takes time to build a strong leadership team for a new business, it is a perfect strategy to bring in a group of leaders of a sister company to cover the transition period. Later on, when the new leadership team is ready, the sister company team can easily go back home with a solid understanding of the new business and a good relationship with the new leaders of the business.

3 ***Leverage expertise.*** John Keisler, CEO of Sunstone Management, worked in the public sector for almost 20 years. His understanding of city government operations and public-private partnerships was unparalleled. When he joined us to run a private business, his public sector resources immediately became a huge advantage, not only for Sunstone Management but for our sister companies such as ALC. Similarly, Dan Wheeler, CEO of Sunstone Trust Company, was a savvy compliance attorney in the financial industry. His expertise made Sunstone Trust Company a fully compliant business in a highly regulated industry from day one. Moreover, he went on to help build a strong compliance structure for both ALC and Sunstone Management. The ways your experienced leaders can help sister companies cannot be underestimated. They can play a big role in your other businesses and there is never any fee! A solo or serial entrepreneur does not get such benefits.

4 ***Leverage ideas to develop new products/services.*** Not too long ago, Sunstone Trust Company registered a subsidiary to launch a "trust card" product. This is a credit card specifically designed for the trust clients of Sunstone Trust Company. I was so intrigued with this "FinTech" strategy (the term used to refer to creating new technologies for the financial field), that when I sat down with my team to discuss our long-range plans, I decided that ALC could use a similar credit product to strengthen its relationship with our EB-5 clients. In fact, no other bankers or credit card sponsors have developed such a product for high-net-worth immigrants in the beginning of their immigration process, but the demand is huge. I ended up borrowing this credit card idea, not just for ALC, but also for Sunstone Management, which can offer a similar credit card product to its entrepreneur clients.

The lesson is: while different businesses are run differently, one idea can innovate for them all. Parallel entrepreneurs are always in the best position to borrow ideas from one business and use them in another.

5 *Leverage financial strength or credit power.* The biggest challenge for any company in the early stages is undoubtedly the lack of financial strength—no or minimal cash flow, no assets, and most importantly, no credit record.

A true benefit that a parallel entrepreneur can offer to his or her second, third, or fourth business is the financial leverage gained from a successful first business. This can be extremely valuable because any subsequently launched company may not be ready to secure a loan or line of credit from a bank given that their financial profile does not meet underwriting requirements. A financially established "big brother" can bypass the bank loan process and directly offer an inter-company loan or a revolving line of credit to provide the capital to the newer family member. ALC did this for Eritage Resort, Sunstone Management, and Sunstone Trust Company, as well as for Partake Collective, my 5th company. This enabled each of my new companies to launch far more quickly with the financial resources needed.

The 2nd Type of Strategic Thinking

PIVOTING: READINESS TO ALTER YOUR COURSE

Today's world is chaotic and volatile. Even the best-planned projects can fail due to circumstances beyond your control. Trends can change overnight, new competitors with a better product can grab market share, or new or revised government regulations can undermine your plans.

Being able to pivot and quickly shift to a new strategy is a necessary talent for any entrepreneur. As soon as you detect a shift in the market or some external forces that interfere with your business progress, you need to be able to figure out what you can do to survive. This requires remaining calm as you scout the horizon for new opportunities or ways to convert your existing product or service to something that matches the new market needs.

Being able to pivot and quickly shift to a new strategy is a necessary talent for any entrepreneur. As soon as you detect a shift in the market or some external forces that interfere with your business progress, you need to be able to figure out what you can do to survive. This requires remaining calm as you scout the horizon for new opportunities or ways to convert your existing product or service to something that matches the new market needs.

It is often not easy to pivot. You need to have an open mind to new possibilities and not get stuck in your past. People are often resistant to change, even if it means the company will not survive, so your team has to be willing to change their thinking, their work culture, and even learn something new. Moreover, you may need to invest in new personnel or new equipment to make the new idea work, expenses that you had not planned on.

I learned about the value of being able to pivot during the Covid pandemic. When Covid first hit in March 2020, ALC was managing a large loan portfolio that was performing extremely well. The monthly repayments of those loans created a strong cash flow that ALC was able to grow upon. Unfortunately, over 70% of the ALC borrowers were hospitality operators. With the Covid lockdowns and subsequent traveling and lodging restrictions launched by the US government, these borrowers were simply in unprecedented big trouble. The termination or reduction of their revenue therefore created an insurmountable hurdle for keeping up with the monthly loan payments. Many borrowers had to stop paying ALC.

To make matters worse, the US government required all lenders to suspend receiving payments for at least six months, thus taking the foreclosure option completely off the table. As a result, ALC lost not only a significant amount of its cash flow, but also the loss recovery rights.

What happened next saved ALC because we were able and willing to pivot. Since the pandemic was affecting millions of companies across the US, the federal government reacted by creating the CARES Act to provide low rate loans and grants to small businesses. One aspect of this legislation was known as the Paycheck Protection Program (PPP), designed to be administered by the SBA in conjunction with banks whose role was to screen and approve the applicants according to certain qualifications. Even better, these loans were intended to be 100% forgiven if the recipient company paid the employees within a certain time period. PPP was intended to keep millions of struggling companies in business so they could pay their workers and keep the economy going during the pandemic. Meanwhile, participating banks would earn fees from SBA on processing the loans.

In the summer of 2020, just when ALC's cash flow loss was reaching 80%, I thought our business was about to finish. Was there any way I could save ALC?

I heard about the CARES Act, and immediately thought of how I started ALC based on the ARRA legislation in 2009. An incredible crisis, Congress passing a new law to correct the ship—it sounded familiar. My intuition was that the CARES Act probably offered exactly what we needed. No surprise, I found the PPP embedded in the legislation.

I realized that here was an opportunity for ALC to pivot and create a new profit center if we were allowed to participate in the program. I tracked the legislation as it went through Congress. When it was finally signed into law, I read the entire PPP language just as I had read the entire ARRA Act under President Obama. I then read the SBA guidelines for PPP that came out on the heels of the CARES Act.

In the first version of the SBA guidelines, nonbank lending institutions such as ALC were not included as eligible participating lenders of the program. But the door seemed to stay open. Every morning after that, I got up and jumped on the SBA website, looking for any updates of the PPP guidelines. A week later, a critical update showed up—SBA included some eligibility requirements for nonbank participants such as ALC that had a lending track record under the SBA programs and their overall financial readiness. Wow! My heart raced with excitement.

I wasted no time completing the application and supporting documents on the same day. The package was submitted right away to the SBA. I made sure we were the first nonbank PPP lender application the government agencies received.

Fortunately, ALC had built an impeccable track record pre-Covid. We had done a great job operating hundreds of SBA 504 loans with EB-5 capital. I had been honored with a national award, "SBA 504 Lender of the Year," in 2017. SBA paid attention to this, as within days they approved my application and passed it to the Department of the Treasury. It took two more months for Treasury to complete its review and give us the green light. On June 8, 2020, when I finally received the approval letter in an email from SBA, I was crying quietly. ALC was saved.

It turned out that ALC was the only PPP lender approved by SBA and Treasury that was nonbank, non-FinTech, and non-Community Development Financial Institution (CDFI). I seized on this new opportunity immediately. If ARRA had given me the chance to launch ALC, the CARES Act helped me save and rebuild our organization.

By the time the CARES program ended in the summer of 2021, ALC had processed and funded approximately 30,000 PPP loans for small businesses across all 50 states of the US. Among the more than 5,000 PPP lenders, the majority of which were banks, ALC was ranked #42 in terms of the total number of PPP loans funded. In effect, ALC was like David compared to the Goliath banks that normally handle nearly all the business under these types of federal government lending programs. ALC shocked the banking world and financially moved to the next level.

How did we achieve that? ALC had only a small team of 12 full-time employees, none of whom had experience handling similar lending programs. They had no training on PPP processing, and no one knew how to market the program, fund the loans, and service them. They also had no IT support system, and worst of all everyone had to work from home under Covid. We therefore knew we all had to work hard and collaborate together to make the program work.

In the end, my team came through; they were not resistant to the change, and in fact embraced learning new things from the PPP program. My staff and team proved to be nimble and flexible, quickly learning how to process these loans and help our clients navigate through the complicated process. The point is, you need to use strategic pivoting when it comes to redirecting your efforts when business throws you a curve.

The 3rd Type of Strategic Thinking

INNOVATION

Leveraging and pivoting are two elements of strategic thinking, but there is a third one: innovation. In my experience, innovation is more than just noticing opportunities to exploit, because innovating requires developing totally new concepts, processes, methods, and/or systems to fulfill those opportunities. In that sense, innovation demands strategic thinking along with a creative mind.

Innovation is more than just noticing opportunities to exploit, because innovating requires developing totally new concepts, processes, methods, and/or systems to fulfill those opportunities. In that sense, innovation demands strategic thinking along with a creative mind.

USING INNOVATION TO CREATE
MY 5TH COMPANY

My fifth company, Partake Collective, was born out of strategic thinking employed to innovate one industry: the restaurant business. Let
me relate the story of how I got the insight to create the new business
concept that Partake Collective represents. Then I will talk about how
I use innovation in my other companies.

In 2019, I was a member of the Economic Development Commission
of Long Beach, California. This commission's purpose was to study
economic problems of the city and attempt to provide recommendations to the city council and mayor. In one of our monthly meetings,
we were focused on studying an astonishing phenomenon happening
among the restaurants in the city: approximately 30% of them had
closed in the past year. How could this be, we asked?

The Commission invited a few of the affected restaurant owners to
the meeting. Each of them shared their story with the commissioners.
As we heard the stories, the picture became clear: we had entered
a new era where family and individual dining habits had significantly
changed. Beginning in the early 2010s, when several mobile phone
applications began to offer a function to order food online, busy people saw a new opportunity to save time. These applications acceler-
ated the development of a new industry: food delivery. Today we are
familiar with many of these companies: Grubhub, Door Dash, Uber
Eats, Postmates, and others. The delivery companies approached
restaurant owners with their prescient new business model—take-out
food delivery services to a growing audience of super-busy families
and young Gen Y and Gen Z diners. However, they presented their
offer to the restaurants with one caveat: to compensate the companies for their deliveries, they asked restaurant owners to raise their
prices by 20%–25% to cover their costs and taxes.

It was a new concept, but it ran up restaurant costs and came with a
lot of uncertainty. Most restaurant owners, being not extremely tech

savvy, were adamantly against the idea and declined the offers. They were unfamiliar with the online business model, and worse, they were blind to innovation. Consumers were hooked on take-out delivery services, but many restaurant owners did not see the writing on the wall.

By around 2020, food delivery had become so massively common and popular that brick-and-mortar restaurant dining areas were nearly empty most of the time. The costly economics of owning a restaurant with lots of wasted dining space and many servers no longer made sense. More and more restaurants in Long Beach struggled to make it, and many were finally forced to close their doors.

As our Economic Development Commission sought to determine how we might help solve this problem, I realized that here was an opportunity to innovate the restaurant industry. If what mattered to the public was the ability to order quality food for delivery, then the only thing that restaurants needed to have was a kitchen with a website/mobile application. A dining area was of little use. In essence, food for take-out could be prepared anywhere there was just a stove, oven, cookware, and enough space to prep and cook the food.

This insight prompted an immediate business idea. I did some research on the emerging concept of "ghost" or cloud/virtual kitchens. A ghost kitchen is essentially a building with dozens of kitchens where food from a wide assortment of restaurants can be prepared and offered for take-out through the delivery app companies. Chefs everywhere might jump at the chance to rent these cooking spaces. This seems to be a real solution for a struggling industry.

And so Partake Collective was born, an innovative ghost kitchen concept that provides entrepreneurial chefs a lower-cost alternative to owning or leasing unnecessary dine-in space for a public that no longer wants to (or can) go out; they welcome the opportunity to obtain and eat restaurant food at home.

Getting Partake Collective off the ground was challenging. In 2020, we purchased an old office building in downtown Long Beach and began modifying it later that year. In our strategic development process, to ensure that we could be steps ahead of a few competitors who were also pursuing the ghost kitchen concept, we sought to innovate the concept with more unique features:

1 In addition to the many separate kitchen units that chefs can lease in the building, we designed a communal kitchen with many workstations that can be rented out on a short-term basis. The rationale for this is that in every community there are large groups such as churches, camps, and other community organizations who need to rent kitchen space to prepare meals for events they are hosting. Our communal kitchens can also be used for food preparation by businesses wanting to test out new products that must be made in an official commercial kitchen to meet the government's food preparation regulations.

2 Ironically, we also decided to include dine-in restaurant space for the public to use like a "super food court." While restaurants were increasingly going out of business, we knew that many diners truly prefer to eat out, and sometimes to be where the action is. In our food court, diners can enjoy meals from the dozens of chefs in the building. Going beyond the framework of food courts in a typical shopping mall, Partake's dine-in experience would be more like an international culinary tour of top chefs cooking foods from around the world. This food court also allows each member of a group or family to choose their own meal, mitigating the stress of the perennial debate families encounter, "Can't we agree on who wants to eat what tonight?"

3 Finally, we created an "incubator" program for restaurateurs who need training in this new business model of food prepared largely for delivery. Our mission is to help our chef-tenants learn about food costing, accounting, and safe food preparation habits. Our research also showed that many take-out meals contain ingredients that do not fit well into the delivery model. Our trainers will thus help chefs learn how to modify their recipes so that the food lasts during the delivery time and tastes great when finally consumed.

Partake Collective's innovative ghost kitchen concept has already become a successful enterprise. The kitchens in our first building in Long Beach were nearly all leased out in advance of the formal business opening in 2022. A second Partake site, located in Los Angeles, was under construction just as the first site in Long Beach started operations. Our goal is to install Partake ghost kitchen buildings in cities throughout the US — giving young chefs opportunities to become entrepreneurs of their own making.

Innovation is critical in every business I own. I believe innovation is the most powerful weapon for startups, providing a clear and immediate competitive advantage against bigger and stronger competitors. In Partake's case, there is not much leveraging; rather, there is a disruptive concept everyone today seems to accept given what happened under Covid restrictions. I am betting on the big trend of dining style change, which I expect to take Partake to great success sooner or later.

Innovation is the most powerful weapon for startups, providing a clear and immediate competitive advantage against bigger and stronger competitors.

Interview with Adam Carrillo, CEO, Partake Collective

How did you become involved with Partake Collective?

Adam Carrillo

I had been an economic development manager for Long Beach and so I knew John Keisler. He and I had discussed for a long time how we had a gap between education and developing some entrepreneurship traction in the city. We believed that Long Beach could be that catalyst for entrepreneurship, but we didn't know what it would look like. At one point, I launched the Long Beach Women's Business Accelerator, and we gave away $40,000 each year, but the startups did not really go anywhere. I also did a lot of work with Long Beach and Cal State in launching their pitch competitions.

I eventually met John Shen when he was discussing with John Keisler and Wade Martin about the development of the Long Beach Accelerator. John asked me to moderate some of the panels about startups for ALC and Sunstone Management.

When John Shen developed the idea for Partake Collective, he asked me to provide support based on my experience and skills in terms of launching a startup, raising capital, real estate investment, and also being able to help the individual businesses involved in the kitchens.

What did it take to launch your first Partake Collective?

We are just in the process of opening it as John Shen writes this book. It was a fairly lengthy development process. We purchased a building in 2020 and sank a hefty amount of money into its renovation. We constructed various kitchen sizes and types and made each one fully ready to lease, providing all the electrical, gas, and plumbing connections necessary. As soon as we started marketing the premises, the demand was strong. Nearly all the commercial kitchens were leased out within months.

Tell us more about how the ghost kitchen concept works.

Our business model began initially with the idea that we would have a home for Michelin-rated chefs, but we realized that our market was really the local "makers and bakers" of the future, the goal being to create a sustainable startup restaurant focused on take-out delivery. We are especially oriented to attracting those who normally have no opportunity to open a restaurant, such as minority and women chefs and restaurateurs.

Our infrastructure makes it easier for them to get started and then to be successful. We arranged an expedited permitting process with the City of Long Beach so that a kitchen can be open in two to four weeks after signing their first one-year lease. Their entry-level costs are low, as all they need to purchase and install are the appliances for their cooking style.

Our goal is to help these chef entrepreneurs succeed for the long term—and that means developing their brand, attracting repeat customers, and growing their revenues. For those who have the right qualities, we will also be assisting them in finding a path to retail distribution of their food products. To a large extent, this also means that Partake itself has a goal to make ourselves excellent partners supporting these makers and bakers through our own marketing and the brand development of Partake Collective itself.

What are your long-term goals?

Pursuant to John Shen's philosophy of business, we are in this for long-term results, not short-term profits. For the moment, we are focused on opening up the Long Beach kitchens and we purchased a second building near Dodger Stadium in Los Angeles that we are in the process of remodeling. We want to learn from these two experiences how to improve our business model, our marketing, and our support for the chefs before we extend Partake Collective elsewhere. But for the moment, we can say that perhaps in five years, you might see several Partake Collective kitchens in Los Angeles and Orange counties in California, and then we will see what happens after that.

Using Innovations in My Other Businesses

Here are some of the innovations my team and I have created in all our businesses.

INNOVATION IN ALC IN THE PPP PROGRAM

We discussed earlier in this chapter how I pivoted when Covid threatened to put ALC out of business and we were able to create an entirely new revenue stream out of the PPP loans. As I mentioned, ALC processed over 30,000 loans for small businesses across the entire US. We outperformed nearly 5,000 other PPP lenders, ranking #42 in terms of the number of loans we processed.

We were just a small team of 12 full-time employees, so how did we do this? Innovation! Right from the start, what became clear to us was that we needed some new technologies to process hundreds of applications on a daily basis. We thus built a processing portal of our own, which, far from perfect, gave us the capacities we needed. It was the first time I learned that processing loans has a great deal to do with IT infrastructure. We became ten times more efficient than most other banks.

As we processed more applications, some fraudulent ones sneaked in. We improved the system to add more fraud detection functions and artificial intelligence features. Without many of these innovative ideas, ALC would have never been as successful in the PPP campaign.

In 2021, ALC also created another innovation. This originated when President Biden signed the Bipartisan Infrastructure Law called the American Rescue Plan to provide $65 billion to upgrade roads, bridges, rail lines, ports, and communities around the country. One aspect of the infrastructure bill aimed to provide $10 billion to states to fund certain types of small businesses that typically have difficulty obtaining loans, specifically minority-owned businesses, companies in low-income areas, and startups. This Act aimed to offer funds to communities in an effort to boost economic growth in these deserving sectors throughout the US.

As soon as I read the details of this program, I saw a new opportunity for ALC to add yet another service to our portfolio. We immediately applied and won approval to become a lender in what was called the State Small Business Credit Initiative (SSBCI), which was part of the infrastructure bill. This was an innovative extension of our EB-5 business, as it brought in a diverse pool of new clients to whom we could offer loans outside of the SBA 504 program. What's more, these new types of clients offered us an opportunity to leverage Sunstone Management, which scouts out the best new startups to invest in, as well as leveraging Partake Collective, which attracts restaurateurs who typically need loans to get their business off the ground. By acting fast and capitalizing on the opportunity, ALC thus created an entirely new channel for business loans.

Pivoting to Cross the Swamp: An Update on Sunstone Trust

I have related why resilience is vital to the entrepreneurial character and discussed that one of the key components of strategic thinking is the ability to pivot. As I was about to publish this book, an unexpected economic event took place that required me to be resilient and pivot in a significant way.

After spending several years and a lot of money to obtain the charter required to operate a trust company, we launched Sunstone Trust in 2021. It blossomed quickly. We had a consistent pipeline of clients available to us and we began implementing innovative technology and new ideas about the trust industry. We were also pursuing estab-lishing trust companies in other states.

In March 2023, however, the financial climate in the US experienced an earthquake-sized jolt. I am referring to the collapse of Silicon Valley Bank and Signature Bank, with possibly more failures to come. These events created an enormously detrimental environment for Sunstone Trust, which depended extensively on small and regional banks to invest in this business and use our capabilities for their clients in need of trust services. I foresaw that Sunstone Trust would soon struggle to secure investments and operational support from the banking community. As founder and chair of the board of directors, I realized that I had to put a stop to my "TrustTech" startup. As this book goes to press, Sunstone Trust Company is thus in the process of being acquired by another bank and will end its journey as one of my companies in mid-2023.

This is a lesson in pivoting for all entrepreneurs, especially parallel entrepreneurs. You must be willing to regularly peer into the horizon at social, economic, or political events and take realistic stock of what seismic changes may mean for your business. You need to be resilient and recognize the need to pivot, even if it means losing a business product, service, or an entire company. As I have stated in this book, when you are trying to cross a swamp you may have to veer off course, navigate around obstacles, and sometimes even take a step backward. Losing Sunstone Trust was a step backward for me. However, I am confident that my advice on how to cross the swamp still stands: As long as you keep moving forward, you will eventually reach dry land.

FIRST-GENERATION ENTREPRENEURS: SPECIAL ISSUES REGARDING STRATEGIC THINKING

Like resilience, strategic thinking may be a quality that many first-generation entrepreneurs feel uncomfortable about or that they are lacking in. Not having grown up in the US, they may believe they do not exactly understand how the business culture works and thus they doubt their ability to launch more than a single business. The challenges of starting their first business may have been so overwhelming that just the thought of starting another venture may be off-putting. And worse, the fear and embarrassment of failing not once, but many times, can also weigh heavily on one's psyche. Why take the risk of launching several businesses when you are not even sure you can succeed with one of them?

But be aware that you are not in as much of a disadvantage as you may believe. Just because you were not born in the US does not mean that you cannot develop the skills of strategic thinking. In fact, know that strategic thinking does not come easily to most people anyway. Many natural-born Americans cannot think logically about a sequence of cause-and-effect actions. If A leads to B, then how might you get to C? Strategic thinking is not taught in schools, other than perhaps in MBA programs.

I encourage first-generation entrepreneurs not to write themselves out of a ticket to larger success as a parallel entrepreneur. You have as much opportunity as I did to figure out how to leverage your clients and transform a single business into multiple companies. You too can utilize your expertise to discover opportunities to innovate in your field. Keep your eyes open for trends and markets you can seize upon. Think about how you can leverage existing clients by forming a new business.

John Shen

REFLECTIONS

Consider these questions. Write out your answers or identify a "success buddy" such as a business partner, another entrepreneur, or a spouse or friend with whom you can discuss the questions.

- Are there areas of your enterprise that you can leverage to create an entirely new business?

- Can you leverage your clients, your processes, or your products to create additional revenue?

- Can you leverage your executive staff or any expertise to boost another business?

- What innovations might you be able to create that could lead to another business?

- Are you looking into the horizon at social, economic, and political events to see if there are any significant changes brewing that may require you to pivot? Do you have any ideas about what you might need to do?

CHAPTER 6

Financial Savvy

SAVVY

- From the Portuguese *sabe*, meaning "he knows," and the Latin *sapere*, meaning "to know, to be wise."

- Synonym: wisdom

John Shen

It goes without saying that any entrepreneur must have at least a basic understanding of financial accounting. Whatever field your expertise is in, as an entrepreneur you need to be able to understand a balance sheet, income statement, and cash flow statement. These documents are the fundamentals of knowing how well your company is doing at any given moment in time as well as on a periodic basis.

But this chapter is not aimed at teaching you the fundamentals of accounting. It is about what I consider the financial secrets that make a startup successful and sustainable. I learned these secrets through trial and error during my Entrepreneurship 1.0, 2.0, and 3.0 phases of my career, and I can attest to their effectiveness. As you recall, I experienced the complete collapse of my real estate business in Florida—and needless to say, that failure taught me harsh financial lessons as well. If you adhere to the advice in this chapter, I am confident you will develop what I call "financial savvy."

Focus on Revenues, Not Profits

The first financial secret, contrary to common thought, is that you need to focus initially on maximizing revenues, not on reaping profits. There is a valid reason behind this maxim: you cannot survive without cash. When I use the term *cash*, I am literally referring to actual money in your bank account, not to the cash flow statement which includes non-cash ghost accounts such as depreciation, accounts receivable, inventory balances, and so on. You cannot pay real-life expenses with accounting ghost accounts, although they are important when your accountant creates the cash flow statement.

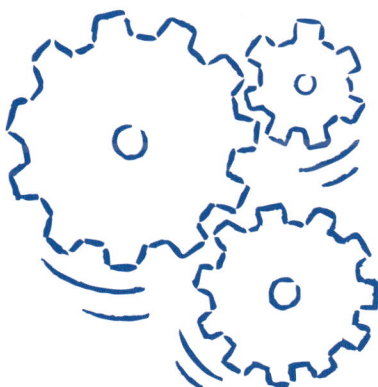

Cash is the lifeblood of any business.
Without revenues, you don't have cash.

Without actual revenues generating cash, you do not have money to pay your expenses—salaries, office space, insurance, cost of goods sold, marketing, taxes, and so on. Without sufficient cash, you will fail to stay in business. I therefore suggest this rule of thumb: stay focused strictly on your revenue growth for at least a few years until your cash reserves are enough to fund all your expenses for at least six months. This provides the cash cushion a new business needs.

Many investors fail to understand this accounting priority. They are oriented towards seeing the business produce *profits* for them, but this is a serious misdirection. Even if you don't have investors, you alone may be focusing too much of your effort trying to produce profits rather than revenues, believing that accumulating profits will attract new investors (as well as making you rich). The problem with this thinking is that you may get a little bit of profit initially, but if the business loses opportunities to generate a lot of revenue, it is more likely to go under and your fountain of profits will eventually dry up.

There is a difference in how you operate a business when your goal is to create revenue rather than profit. Let's say it takes 30 minutes to sell your product or service to a customer and the sale brings in $300 in revenue, and $75 in profit. On average, say you can make 14 sales a day, thus $4,200 per day in revenue, and $1,050 in profit.

Compare that to a scenario in which you want to increase profits, so you raise the price to $900, which allows you to make $400 in profit. But, with this higher price, it takes you longer to make each sale. Say it now takes you two hours to sell the same product to a client (you have to meet them, spend time chatting, persuade them to buy, etc.), rather than 30 minutes; now you can make only four sales per day, bringing in just $3,600 in revenue, but $1,600 in profit.

Comparison of Focusing on Revenue vs. Profit

	Focus on revenue	Focus on profit
Product price	$300	$900
Profit	$75	$400
Time needed to sell	30 minutes	2 hours
Average sales per 8 hour day	14	4
Total revenue per day	**$4,200**	$3,600
Total profit per day	$1,050	**$1,600**

As this example illustrates, when your eye is on maximizing profit, not revenue, you are losing $600 per day in revenue, despite making an extra $550/day in profit. Over 20 business days per month, you are losing $600/day, thus $12,000/month. Over several months, the loss of tens of thousands in revenue may be sufficient to force you into bankruptcy, given that you do not have enough cash to pay expenses. Yes, someone made a nice profit in that time frame, but it was short-lived.

The point is, when you calculate your product or service pricing, you need to think about the time it takes you to make a sale at a given price and then select a price that helps you maximize your revenue from sales, not your profits. Time is money, but revenues represent the cash you need to stay in business and become sustainable.

There is a great advantage to making your product or service the most competitive in your marketplace when your goal is to maximize revenue, not profit. If you can sell at a lower price, despite a lower profit margin, it helps you sell your product or service faster, in less time, and you are more likely to sell more per day. This gives you the opportunity to grow your business faster and attract more attention in your marketplace so you can earn a bigger market share and better control of the market—a big advantage to a new startup.

If you can sell at a lower price, despite a lower profit margin, it helps you sell your product or service faster, in less time, and you are more likely to sell more per day. This gives you the opportunity to grow your business faster and attract more attention in your marketplace . . .

John Shen

The Faucet and Tub Analogy to Business Growth

Imagine that your venture is like a tub with a faucet pouring water into it. At the bottom is a drain allowing water to escape.

The faucet is your stream of revenue; the drain is the outflow of cash to pay your expenses. At any given moment, the faucet is flowing at the same rate as the drain leaks out water. No water sits in the tub. This means you have no net profit.

But assume you can increase the flow from the faucet, meaning you increase your revenue. If the drain still outflows at the same rate, the tub will fill up little by little and the water level will rise. When that happens, you can put some fish in the tub and they will survive.

That's the value of prioritizing revenue, not profit. It allows you build up your cash flow to create extra cash to do things with. With more cash, you can invest in more inventory, hire more staff, spend more on marketing and PR, and build your brand. In short, revenues fill your tub and allow you to go fishing.

This rationale may seem counterintuitive to entrepreneurs focused on profits. I am always astonished when entrepreneurs insist they cannot lower their profit margins yet they know that they are losing opportunities to sell more units and create enough revenue to survive. They are like owners of a sinking yacht; they enjoyed the wealth while it lasted, but when the business goes under, they have nothing left.

My experience is that when a company grows its revenue enough to succeed, it becomes far easier to modify your profit margin at a later stage. My fundamental logic is this: grow the company as fast as possible based on revenues so you can "buy time" to organize your business, establish your brand, and create a customer base you can leverage.

Pick the Best Workplace

Choosing a workplace usually is the biggest long-term financial commitment a startup makes on day one. This decision has both an immediate and a long-term impact on every single aspect of one's business. It largely determines who has the best chances of getting involved and making contributions to the business: i.e., potential employees, business partners, and most importantly, customers. Secondly, it affects most items in your operating budget: rent, equipment, utilities, travel costs, and so on. Once a specific workplace is locked in, a large portion of your operating budget is mostly set. Finally, I believe every workplace has a certain vibe that helps establish the character and culture of your business. As part of one's local business community, a startup always carries something of the flavor of that community, which, in the long run, can have a significant influence on its success. As for entrepreneurs who follow the principles of feng shui, that can play a role too, a topic outside the scope of this book.

One typical mistake many early-stage companies make is choosing a workplace based on low cost. Even though saving money is important,

I strongly suggest that you not treat cost as the deciding factor if you can afford something a little better.

Some entrepreneurs simply choose a location near their home; although this might make sense in terms of keeping the cost of commuting down, it's not a good idea if it does not help you attract stakeholders. If it is a temporary lease deal, such as for just six months or a year, it is probably fine. However, if the lease is for three or five years, the business owner must take into consideration many factors and decide carefully.

I chose to move from Florida to Southern California to start ALC back in 2010 as I believed it was the best decision for my new company. California, especially Southern California, has been the gateway of most new immigrants from Asia for decades and therefore is the best place to meet and entertain them and their agents. As I had to travel frequently to East Asian countries like China, Los Angeles made the most sense, since it is the US city that has the most flights to these countries. There were so many reasons supporting my decision to relocate to Southern California that this decision was a no-brainer.

My first office was in the World Trade Center in Long Beach. I spent more than 11 years (2010–2021) in that same building. This was not a problem in the 2010s. I enjoyed working and living in the city of Long Beach.

Then when ALC began growing quickly and my second, third, and fourth companies launched one after another in the pre-pandemic years, I decided I had to look for a bigger, more appropriate stage for them. I felt we needed a more diversified community; one that favors financial services and innovation would make a better home for my businesses. In 2021, I chose to relocate to Irvine, a Southern California city named as one of America's safest cities for 16 years in a row until 2021 (based on FBI Uniform Crime Reporting statistics) and also a leading North American city in tech job growth, as noted by a Global Commercial Real Estate Services report in 2021. I am grateful that we made this move, as all of my four California-based companies have thrived since our move there.

Go for Organic Growth

UNLESS YOUR BUSINESS TRULY QUALIFIES FOR INVESTMENT...

Many startups begin through self-funding (a.k.a. bootstrapping), by which I mean using their own savings and perhaps credit cards to pay expenses for an initial period until they have cash from operations. Self-funding is the easiest and least complicated method of launching a new business. The biggest advantage is that you are not indebted to other people, financially or psychologically. You are not compelled to listen to anyone's advice on how to run your company. You do have any stress about being unable to pay investors back. And you are free to pursue revenue growth without producing a profit for others to take away from you.

Self-funding is not possible for every entrepreneur, however Your venture may require hundreds of thousands of dollars, or even millions, to launch, putting it out of range for self-funding. Or you may not even have the small sum of $10,000 or $20,000 to get a simple business off the ground.

Depending on the amount you need, you have various options to involve investors. First, the easiest and often quickest method of funding with investors is to tap into family and friends. Personal loans engender less paperwork and avoid the documentation and legal filings required when seeking funding from professional investors.

However, there are caveats galore when you borrow from family and friends. Their closeness to you invites them to feel they can give you advice, even if they have no idea how your business works. The psychological burden on you to pay them back creates strain and stress. Fear that you cannot pay them back if things go awry can make just normal get-togethers with them uncomfortable. In the event that your business fails and you cannot pay them back, their reaction will remain a perennial shroud over your former relationship with them.

As I related, after my Florida real estate business collapsed in 2008, I had to call my parents in China and ask for financial assistance. They sent me their entire life savings, $30,000, which allowed me to support my family through 2009 and 2010. However, that was not enough for launching my new ALC business, a complicated business model.

Fortunately, I was able to reach out to a few close friends, who helped me raise another $30,000 to cover some critical expenses in the preparation for the regional center proposal I had to submit to USCIS. During the first six months of the operation, I also had to borrow an additional $50,000 from a friend, and eventually paid him back. Since I did the majority of the work myself in launching ALC, the money I raised from my family and friends was sufficient to cover my expenses.

In those early years, I had no knowledge of how to raise funds from angel investors or VC firms. I also would have had a hard time explaining to anyone the complicated ALC model anyway. As the business generated profits, I reinvested them back into the business. In this way, I have never had to raise capital for ALC from any investors other than friends and family. The growth of ALC has been exclusively fueled by its own profits. This is true organic growth.

So is it better or worse to self-fund and grow organically? Is it worth it to seek investors?

In most cases, I believe, if you are rich enough—or your family and friends are capable of funding your business venture for at least several years—you do NOT need to chase money in the investor community. Raising capital systematically takes a huge toll on your business. You can easily spend more than 50% of your precious time on fundraising, and still end up with nothing. If you succeed in raising investor funding, you must accept a diluted ownership arrangement, leading eventually to less control over your business while constantly handling investor expectations.

Today's venture capital market is becoming so competitive, early-stage investments only go to the most innovative and disruptive concepts and great management teams. If you operate a regular brick-and-mortar shop, you have almost no chance. But if you have an eye-opening idea or a unique business model, you have a good opportunity to sign up investors. Sunstone Trust Company and Partake Collective are good examples of startup businesses that needed systematic fundraising and got it. Although I could not raise funds for ALC, and I used my ALC profits to fund Eritage and Sunstone Management, both Sunstone Trust Company and Partake Collective were precisely the types of candidates that investors seek out.

If you are rich enough—

or your family and friends are

capable of funding your business

venture for at least several years—

you do NOT need to chase money

in the investor community.

Raising capital systematically

takes a huge toll on your business.

Glossary of Investment Terms

Understanding the investment world is a necessary component of being an entrepreneur. It can be confusing to know where to turn to raise funding for your venture, as each type of investment has its advantages and disadvantages. Here is a quick overview of the types of investors that entrepreneurs usually turn to.

Early-stage pre-seed money. This refers to the earliest money you may receive from friends and family to get your business off the ground. These people may not get an equity position in the company; they are usually just paid back for their investment and thanked.

Angel money. Angel investors are those who swoop in to help you, but their investments are usually minimal. Angels may include friends and family, but there are increasingly professional angels and angel groups to whom you can pitch. Angel funding is usually in the tens or hundreds of thousands, not in the millions. Angels expect to be repaid as soon as the business takes off or obtains other investors. Some angel deals involve a SAFE, Simple Agreement for Future Equity, by which the company agrees to let the angels buy stock shares at a guaranteed price when the company offers equity shares.

Turn Crisis into Opportunity

Without knowing the details of your business—i.e., what products or services you offer, your market conditions, how long you have been in business—it is difficult to recommend how you might catch or create opportunities to grow your business. However, there is one significant growth opportunity for every business that most of us normally ignore. It occurs when there is a Big Crisis of some kind. The bigger the crisis appears to be, the more opportunities you can possibly seize to grow your business. Why is this?

Seed money investors. This term relates to the first round of profit-oriented investors who seek to fund an existing venture with a minimum viable product (MVP) that shows signs of commercial success. Seed investors may put in from $25,000 to $2 million each in exchange for an ownership stake in the business, from 7% to 10%.

Venture Capital (VC). VC companies invest large sums ranging from $1 million to $20 million into established startups that have gone beyond just having an MVP to demonstrating a highly successful revenue model and a growing base of customers. Their goal is to gain equity shares of the company at low cost in this early stage and reap substantial appreciation over time as the company's stock multiplies in value. Venture capital is usually offered in rounds, called Series A, B, C, and sometimes D.

Equity Crowdfunding. The innovation of crowdfunding has taken the world by storm in the past decade. Crowdfunding platforms for entrepreneurs invite anyone to invest in a startup in exchange for a small amount of equity shares. Some crowdfunding platforms are aimed at entrepreneurs who seek larger amounts from syndicates of investors who pool their money to gain leverage on the venture's equity.

Crisis means something is not right that requires someone to develop a solution. And therein lies the opportunity.

After my real estate business failure in Florida, I hit rock bottom and could not imagine how to resuscitate that business. The US economy in 2008 was devastated; the real estate market in shambles; it was an economic crisis almost as severe as the Great Depression. I knew I had to discover or invent a different business to enter. But what?

As I recounted earlier in the book, for some reason I had the intuitive sense that I should read the American Recovery and Reinvestment Act (ARRA) to see if it might contain ideas. Perhaps it was my Chinese background that taught me if you look hard enough, you can spot opportunities in crisis. It was the ARRA legislation that led me to realize I could merge the EB-5 program with the SBA 504 loan program, and this became the foundation for ALC.

I also related in the previous chapter that I did the same thing after the pandemic was about to close down ALC, when the majority of our clients, composed of hotels and restaurants, could not pay off their monthly loan premiums due to their own lack of business. The economic disaster facing millions of small businesses forced the Federal government to create the CARES Act, which funded the PPP loan program for qualifying small businesses. I was able to take advantage of the pandemic crisis by reading the CARES Act and paying attention to the SBA component that was involved in administering the loans. I saw that ALC could become a lender in the program and thus the PPP loans created an entirely new revenue stream for ALC.

The point I suggest you take from this is: in order to be a savvy entrepreneur with a sustainable business, you must keep looking for ways to grow your revenue, and sometimes this needs to be a completely new way to generate revenue. How to do that can often be discovered by reflecting on whatever crisis might be occurring in society, in your industry, or among your clients. Crisis means something is not right and needs a solution. Think about what your venture can do to provide that solution.

Do not panic when crisis hits. Seek out ways to leverage, pivot, or innovate new solutions.

As CEO or a senior executive in your startup, you have to be among those who remain calm and rational. Emotional reactions and assumptions born out of stress and worry can often drive owners and their executive teams to make hasty decisions that end up in disaster for the company. Slow things down and use your intellect to analyze the situation. Somewhere in the crisis, whatever it is, you will find an opportunity to leverage, pivot, or innovate to help your business grow, or at least prevent it from completely folding.

Reduce the Risk of Failure via Diversification

I cannot understate the need to ensure that your venture does not rely on just one revenue stream. It is essential to diversify your businesses across several product or service lines. If you are a parallel entrepreneur, the best overall strategy is to diversify your portfolio of

I cannot understate the need to

ensure that your venture does not

rely on just one revenue stream.

It is essential to diversify your

businesses across several product

or service lines. If you are a parallel

entrepreneur, the best overall

strategy is to diversify your portfolio

of businesses so you can operate

in different industries.

businesses so you can operate in different industries. Diversification protects your risk if any one product, service line, or entire business encounters a crisis or starts to collapse on its own.

I've discussed how ALC was born out of the merger I made between soliciting foreign investors under the EB-5 program and matching their money with small business loans ALC made under the SBA 504 program. I am fully aware, however, of a fatal flaw in this business model. What if the federal government withdraws the EB-5 program? That would dry up nearly all of the loan business that ALC performs. In fact, our other loan product line, PPP loans, ended in 2021, leaving ALC with very little potential to remain a sustainable lender.

Fortunately, thanks to the impeccable lending track record of the last decade, ALC is now able to build credit facilities at a large enough scale to support its broad-based lending practice. Its ever-growing access of the US capital market, especially through the US banking community, is offering an alternative capital source outside the EB-5 capital.

Regarding my portfolio of businesses, I have consciously expanded them to diversify the risk in several ways:

- Sunstone Management markets to private high-net-worth clients. It does not depend on the EB-5 program and represents an evergreen market, as the wealth of its clients and potential client families is unlikely to disappear.

- The operation of Sunstone Management is not subject to the risk of any federal immigration policy change.

- Neither Eritage Resort nor Partake is involved in the financial sector nor is either solely dependent on high-net-worth clients seeking to invest. Both are involved in the evergreen food/wine sectors.

Should the US economy collapse again as it did in 2008, it is unlikely that all my companies would all be degraded to the point of total business failure such as happened in 2008 in Florida. To be a parallel entrepreneur, you too need to develop this same degree of financial savvy.

The Big Financial Decision

SELLING OR KEEPING YOUR COMPANY

One of the biggest financial decisions an entrepreneur might need to make is whether to sell your company or not. Is it more financially savvy to accept a buyout offer or to hold on to your company for more years?

There is no one right answer here. The most financially savvy solution depends on each circumstance and the owner's personal frame of mind. Whenever I get a chance to sit down with young entrepreneurs, part of my conversation is related to asking them about their vision, especially their long-term goals. A frequent scenario is that the founder of an early-stage startup comes to me because they receive a buyout offer and they don't know what to do. They want to know if they should sell. If they accept the buyout offer, their working days could literally be over. They sell their company and it ends a major chapter of their life.

However, I point out to them that if they believe they can dominate a sector or make a big change in their community, they should keep the business and grow it. If they are an early market leader, why stop? I encourage them to spend time thinking about their future goals and to develop their sense of vision to spot trends.

Let me point out, however, that sometimes it makes sense for an entrepreneur to sell the business. In some cases, especially when the entrepreneur is asked to stay onboard and head up a subsidiary or a division of the acquiring company, this could be a ticket to even greater success than keeping the company. It is just another version of long-term goals.

Get Professional Advice

YOUR TAX ADVANTAGES

My final secret to being financially savvy is to be sure you consult with good attorneys and corporate accounting professionals, as there are tremendous tax benefits if you structure your multiple companies the right way. For instance, you may be the founder and owner of the companies in spirit, but you can structure the companies so that you are part of the management team in one company, earning a salary and a bonus, while you are the owner in another, and a passive investor in a third. There are many permutations of how to structure your ownership and the role you play in each company.

At the corporate level, you can also structure the tax burden in perfectly legal ways to shift income from one company to another. For instance, if one company makes a lot of money and another doesn't, you can offset taxable income by sharing resources from the money-making company with the one that loses money. Given that tax laws are extremely complex and frequently shifting, I cannot provide any specific advice, so be sure you discuss the many options you might have with a qualified professional.

FIRST-GENERATION ENTREPRENEURS: SPECIAL ISSUES REGARDING FINANCIAL SAVVY

If many American entrepreneurs need to learn my lessons of financial savvy, I have seen that first-generation entrepreneurs are far more beleaguered by them. For one, first-generation founders may have a strong resistance to focusing on revenues, not profits. In their minds, an enterprise is not successful if they cannot show profits to their family and friends. Explaining my logic to family members who grew up and may continue to live in another country is usually incomprehensible to them. The pressure to produce profits may be insurmountable and lead precisely to the problems that I discussed: short-term profits but not enough long-term revenue to stay in business.

Secondly, there also might be resistance to the notion I propose that entrepreneurs give preference to organic growth rather than seeking outside investment. In the American Startup Dream, many first-generation entrepreneurs tend to believe that success means chasing venture capital funding. The allure of being a startup that receives a huge funding investment can make first-generation entrepreneurs move too quickly, without the right planning for what to do with a sizeable investment. Chasing funding can be a real waste of time as well, time that should be spent building the business.

Finally, first-generation entrepreneurs may find it difficult to diversify as I suggest. Many of them earned an advanced university degree in the US and their expertise is narrow. When a crisis occurs that affects their business, they may find it impossible to switch gears to turn that crisis into an opportunity or to evaluate whether they could start another business, as I did with my second company, Eritage Resort.

Financial savvy as I have come to understand it runs counter-intuitive to the way that many Americans think, but it I suggest it can be even harder for first-generation entrepreneurs to come around to my way of thinking. If you are a first-generation entrepreneur, I hope you will read this chapter closely and take it seriously.

REFLECTIONS

Consider these questions. Write out your answers or identify a "success buddy" such as a business partner, another entrepreneur, or a spouse or friend with whom you can discuss the questions.

- What is your background for understanding financial statements? Have you studied financial accounting and do you pay attention to the financial statements or rely on your accountant to interpret them for you?

- Do you put profit ahead of revenue when you create your business goals? Can you see how it could help your company if you changed your mindset to increase your revenue, not your profit?

- Did you start your company using your own funds, those of family and friends, or angel investors? How would you feel if you were unable to pay them back?

- Are your business lines diversified, or if you are operating multiple companies, are they in different industries? Can you find ways to further diversify your products, services, or industries?

- Have you chosen a workplace location? Is it working for you in terms of attracting the best employees, customers, and other stakeholders? Might you be better off somewhere else?

CHAPTER 7

Leadership and Vision

VISION

- From the Latin *videre*, "to see"

- Synonyms: imagination, inventiveness

- Leadership – from old English, "to guide, to conduct"

- Synonyms: supervision, guidance

John Shen

As an entrepreneur, you must be a leader, of course. But what is leadership? What are the qualities of leadership you need for a successful business?

There are actually many theories of leadership. If you were to Google the term "leadership theories," you would find scores of articles and books on the topic. Some state that there are 4 theories of leadership; others discuss 8 theories; still others go into as many as 12 theories. Whichever you believe, here are the 5 leading theories:

- *The "heroic leader" theory.* This is also called the "great person" theory, which says leaders are special people who are born to lead. From birth, they have the qualities of leadership inherent in their genes: intelligence, analytical ability, charm, confidence, and social skills. This theory suggests you cannot learn to be a leader. I disagree.

- *The "special trait" theory.* This is similar to the heroic leader, in claiming that people who have certain traits, such as courage, risk-taking, extroversion, and self-confidence, can become great leaders. The theory appears to suggest that if you develop these traits, you can become a leader. What is unclear about this theory, however, is that there is no complete list of necessary traits. It's confusing and indefinite.

- *The "authoritarian leader" theory.* This is one who leads by building up power over individuals using rewards and punishments. These leaders need to control their company and be at the helm of every decision, no matter how small. Some believe authoritarian leadership is no longer functional in an increasingly democratic world, but many large organizations continue to be led by authoritarians.

- **The "servant leader" theory.** This theory refers to people who can attract followers because they encourage others to do their best work, welcome diversity of thought, aim to create an organizational culture of mutual trust, and do not seek power but rather build up the leadership skills in others. This type of leadership is gaining ground among many young entrepreneurs who do not want to act in an authoritarian manner.

- **The "situational leader" theory.** This is a theory that says leaders need to adjust how they lead according to the situation. There may be conditions when an authoritarian approach is needed, and other situations when being a servant leader works more effectively. We might say that leaders who can do this need to be analytical or intuitive, at the minimum. These leaders recognize the conditions going on around them and are able to adjust their leadership style on the quick.

So what type of leadership is the best one for becoming a solo, serial, or parallel entrepreneur? Here is what I have learned during the three phases of my career.

My Journey to Leadership

When I launched my first real estate business in Florida around 2000, I began simply by earning a real estate license. Initially I did not need to lead anyone; I had no staff. However, I quickly became a broker, a property manager, and a while later I obtained the license to be a mortgage broker. Within a few years I had a large office with a staff of people, and suddenly I had to become a leader.

I knew nothing about leading, though. I was a boss, for sure, but I was not a true leader. I had never studied leadership, nor did I have an MBA. I had not read any books on leadership. And although I held corporate jobs in my past when I worked in the pharmaceutical

LEADERSHIP INSIGHTS

1.

Begin thinking about your leadership development as soon as you are thinking about launching an entrepreneurial adventure. You will need to become a leader eventually.

2.

As an entrepreneurial leader, you must have the knowledge needed to teach others about your business. You must know how to do nearly every job in your company so you can teach your employees.

3.

If you expand your entrepreneurial endeavor to other business sectors you are unfamiliar with, hire someone experienced in that industry or outsource the work to lead the effort.

4.

The entrepreneurial leader must develop the quality of being a visionary. Having the ability to look into the future, recognize trends, and act on them is a critical element of leadership. But it takes more than that. You also need to be able to explain your vision and attract others to follow you in chasing it.

5.

Leadership is a never-ending learning process.

industry, I had no true experience leading people in the way an entrepreneur must who is growing a single company, and I was certainly unprepared to become a leader as a parallel entrepreneur. In some part, it was my lack of diversification and one important leadership skill—vision—that led to my downfall in 2008. I had failed to notice the severity of the real estate crisis brewing on the horizon in 2007.

When I returned to being an entrepreneur and founded ALC in 2009, I still had no inkling about leadership. Starting over again, I became a company consisting of myself and a couple of partners. If you are launching a new enterprise as I did, you may be in this same position; that is to say, you are unaware of your future need to truly step into the role of being a leader. It's just not on your radar.

Unless you are a natural-born leader (see "heroic leader" theory above), I have five insights to share. Here is the first:

LEADERSHIP INSIGHT 1:

Begin thinking about your leadership development as soon as you are thinking about launching an entrepreneurial adventure. You will need to become a leader eventually.

By 2011, ALC had sufficient EB-5 clients to justify hiring support staff to assist me. This was the true start of my journey to learn how to be a leader. I brought in two critical employees, Bruce Thompson and Stella Zhang, and soon offered both shares of the company. The three of us were the management team for ALC for the entire next decade.

As the company continued its growth in size, my staff looked to me to guide them in understanding the EB-5 program and lending business. In addition, each time I hired a new person, I had to personally show them how to do their job. This is my next insight into leadership:

LEADERSHIP INSIGHT 2:

As an entrepreneurial leader, you must have the knowledge needed to teach others about your business. You must know how to do nearly every job in your company so you can teach your employees.

In 2012, we purchased the land in Walla Walla, Washington that eventually became Eritage Resort. Given that we had no experience in wine making or the hospitality industry, we hired a developer to construct the resort building and a management company to operate the resort and vineyard. Of course, we were involved in the decision-making, but it was clear that I could not be the actual leader of the effort to create this business, having no experience in it. My third recommendation is based on this experience with Eritage:

LEADERSHIP INSIGHT 3:

If you expand your entrepreneurial endeavor to other business sectors you are unfamiliar with, hire someone experienced in that industry or outsource the work to lead the effort.

Between 2010 and 2015, I was the CEO of ALC, growing the company to substantial success. By 2015, ALC had more than 20 employees. I was six years into my Entrepreneurship 1.0 phase, and I was finally becoming more confident of my ability to lead people on a day-to-day basis. But my journey to entrepreneurial leadership was just starting. I had ideas to expand ALC and start yet another new company.

In 2015, I founded Sunstone Management and entered my Entrepreneurship 2.0 phase, where I was slowly shifting into being a parallel entrepreneur. With ALC in good stead by now, I was able to spend 70% to 80% of my time working on building that company. Over the course of the next five years, 2015–2020, I led Sunstone Management into becoming a highly respected and recognized fast-growing investment firm. I leveraged some of the staff from ALC to move over to working on Sunstone Management, given that they already had a strong relationship with the people who became clients of both companies.

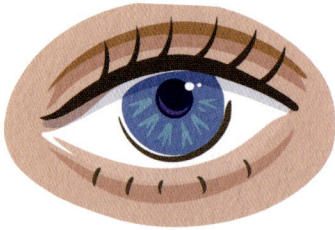

This period of time advanced my leadership abilities to new heights; I was able to hone what I consider one of the key qualities of leadership: being a visionary. This leadership capacity is the basis for my next insight:

LEADERSHIP INSIGHT 4:

The entrepreneurial leader must develop the quality of being a visionary. Having the ability to look into the future, recognize trends, and act on them is a critical element of leadership. But it takes more than that. You also need to be able to explain your vision and attract others to follow you in chasing it.

Since 2017, I have been challenged to become a strong visionary leader, especially as I transitioned into my Entrepreneurship 3.0 phase, that of being a true parallel entrepreneur. To lead multiple companies, you have no choice but to inspire others to understand your vision for success and growth. The normal tasks of leadership magnify in complexity and require the people around you to be fully committed to being "all on the same team." You cannot recruit the best people to assist you if they do not respect your vision and have no interest in pursuing it with you. Looking back at my trajectory since 2009, I know that today I am a completely different leader than I was when my journey began.

If I had to say which leadership theory category I fall into, it would be a hybrid of the servant leader and the situational leader. I am definitely not a "heroic" leader, as I am the first to admit that I was not born with natural leadership skills. I was a shy, introverted child and did not fully grow out of that personality type for decades. Being a first-generation entrepreneur from China and learning to fit into American culture was difficult for me, given how different the customs of my native country are and my personality type.

Today, I operate all my companies by seeking first and foremost to be a visionary leader for everyone. Leading more than 100 employees, as chairman of the board for all my companies and CEO for ALC, I aim to inspire everyone to do their best work, to believe in what we do, and to be committed to growing these enterprises together.

I take pride in knowing all my employees by name, and more importantly, I know their jobs, because I have done most of them. I have an open door policy and welcome anyone to ask me questions (and I can usually answer them). I enjoy learning from other people and am open-minded when there are options for any decision to be made. I believe in being nice to every single employee, in the sense of treating them respectfully and courteously.

But there are circumstances when I must also act according to the situation, which sometimes involves being insistent on having work done the way I want it done. I seldom become angry with others, but I am not afraid of telling people they are wrong.

All in all, my journey to being the leader I am today brings me to a final insight that I firmly believe is true:

LEADERSHIP INSIGHT 5:

Leadership is a never-ending learning process.

It takes time to create your leadership knowledge and style, to step into the real power of leadership. Few people are 100% born leaders. There is always something to learn.

Not having been naturally born a "heroic leader" or "great person" should not deter anyone from choosing to be an entrepreneur. There are many varied personality traits that together can make up an entre-preneurial leader, and you can learn to adopt them into your life and practice them to make them come more naturally to you. These include self-confidence, extroversion, decisiveness, charm, and even charisma. One can learn these qualities, as my life experience attests. I began my journey as a Chinese student immigrant in the US who was shy, introverted, and could barely speak English. Today I am the founder of multiple companies, leading them as best as I can towards the highest level of entrepreneurial success. There is not a day that goes by when I am not learning something new.

Developing Your Leadership Vision

The capacity of a leader to be a visionary is so important to being a suc-cessful entrepreneur that I need to comment at length about it. Vision is for me the key mental task of leadership for the solo or serial entre-preneur, but it is vital if you seek to become a parallel entrepreneur.

A visionary leader sees through the fads and buzzwords of the moment to decipher the real trends.

Leadership Means Being Able to Relate to People in All Tiers of the Company

We usually think of a leader as being the one who decides, the person at the top of the hierarchy. You hold the power to make decisions and to determine the direction your company takes. You have the authority to direct the executive staff, monitor their jobs, conduct high-level meetings, and negotiate contracts.

But I have also talked about how entrepreneurs must be able to do nearly every job in the company. You probably started out working alone and playing every role. You were your own support staff; you have the knowledge for how to do the lower-tier jobs.

A great entrepreneurial leader is able to function at all levels. You should be comfortable leading those occupying the highest tiers of your organization; that is, you are at ease and effective when speaking to CEOs of other companies or hobnobbing with wealthy investors. But you are also just as comfortable speaking with all employees in your firm, being friendly and respectful to everyone, from department heads to secretarial staff, to the cleaning crew and errand-runners.

When you are a parallel entrepreneur, working at all levels is a necessity. Remember: when you launch one company and achieve a level of success, you might be working as a leader most of the time. But as soon as you launch your next company, you may need to return to working in the trenches, doing every job needed to get that company going since you cannot afford to hire anyone. On some days, you may be CEO of your first company in the morning and secretary or mailroom clerk of your second company in the afternoon.

*Being a leader gives you a commanding perspective of your field.
People are eager to listen to your ideas.*

I suggest that developing vision is a function of gaining experience in an industry. You need to have many years of experience under your belt to develop a good understanding of where your industry is headed. You must be able to distinguish fads from trends, and know what directions the industry is most likely going in. Having keen vision allows you to be the first to catch a wave, and to make adjustments in your business to capitalize on it.

I suggest that being a parallel entrepreneur actually helps develop one's visionary capabilities far more than the entrepreneur who owns a single company. Parallel entrepreneurs have exposure to many industries and trends, which accelerates your visionary capacities. You learn to see business holistically rather than in narrow tranches. If you are a serial entrepreneur, working in one specific sector, you are doing one thing at a time in just a single field. It's hard to see outside your sector.

But when you are a parallel entrepreneur, you simultaneously run different businesses in multiple sectors. This enables you to scout a wider horizon across many vistas. Visioning about your businesses becomes

Being a parallel entrepreneur

actually helps develop one's

visionary capabilities far more

than the entrepreneur who

owns a single company.

Parallel entrepreneurs have

exposure to many industries

and many trends,

which accelerates your

visionary capacities.

a skill you can then naturally apply to other areas you are exploring. You can more easily discern trends in other industries because you are familiar with other sectors.

I knew nothing about the restaurant business when I served on the Long Beach Economic Development Commission and we listened to a presentation about the closing of 30% of the city's restaurants due to the take-out delivery business. But I had already worked enough in the financial industry to realize that I was looking squarely at a paradigm shift in the restaurant industry. I predicted the next wave of the food business would be in the ghost kitchen concept—and I decided to catch that wave before others did. If I had not created Partake, another entrepreneur would have. I could see the void, and I am convinced that Partake will be one of the winners in this new food sector.

If you are not a visionary and believe you cannot develop that skill, you might consider hiring a talented individual as your Chief Visionary Officer (CVO). Their task is to scout the horizons, looking for trends, and report them to you as CEO. Having a CVO onboard is not unusual; many large corporations employ one.

The Ideal Triumvirate of Leadership in a Technical Startup

Many startups today are in technical fields, led by entrepreneurs with a technical background. As "techies," they are super-skilled in their field, and their innovative ideas becomes the foundation of their startups.

What such techies often lack, though, is vision. They are focused solely on the technical advancement of their own product or service. They cannot take a wider holistic view of their industry and see where the trends are going. Their talent in technology may drive their venture to succeed and then be sold to another firm at great profit. But their lack of vision means they remain one-hit entrepreneurs at worst, or perhaps serial entrepreneurs at best if they manage to start another company.

A view of the uniquely designed space inside Partake Long Beach

As cited earlier, Sunstone Management sponsors a number of startup pitch competitions, such as the Sunstone Innovation Challenge, and invests in the cohort members of many accelerators. We often see this vision problem among tech firms whose young leaders are exceptional techies, but they lack visionary skills. My company often becomes involved in advising those tech startups, taking a role on their board of directors or providing hands-on consulting to the executive team.

I have thought long and hard about tech startups and have come to this conclusion: Given that technical entrepreneurs tend to lack vision skills, I suggest that the ideal formation of a tech venture include a triumvirate executive team composed of the technical entrepreneur, a chief visionary officer (CVO), and an expert chief financial officer (CFO). These are the three key positions that can make technical startups succeed.

Hiring and Retaining the Right People Requires Vision

There is another critical reason that entrepreneurial leadership requires exceptional visionary skills—hiring exceptional people to work with you. You need high-quality individuals to be part of your team for each of your companies. As your company grows, you may need to secure a CEO, a VP, or a partner. If you are founding a new company, you might need to hire a new CEO while you focus on the new venture.

The problem is, when you are just a small startup, it is impossible to compete with larger, stronger corporations in your area when it comes to recruiting. When you are in the early stages of a startup, you seldom have the resources to pay the salaries that top talents want and can easily obtain elsewhere.

Given this limitation, being a visionary plays a key role in being able to hire the right people. Every job interview you do must be a "vision talk" that motivates the potential candidate. You have to be able to paint an inspiring picture of your company and its future. Your vision speech needs to appeal to their emotions and gently persuade them that one's work is not always about reaping immediate money if better rewards are available in the future. While you cannot offer them the kind of salary + benefits package they might get from an established player, your vision talk lures them with tales of your company's great work culture, the exciting challenges they will have in their job, and the potential of substantial monetary compensation once your company achieves its expected success. Every current executive and employee who interviews a potential candidate must share that same vision with them. Every interview by every employee with a candidate is an opportunity to show how this powerful vision is shared. Everyone must be synchronized.

Being a visionary plays a key role in being able to hire the right people. Every job interview you do must be a "vision talk" that motivates the potential candidate.

STRATEGIES FOR HIRING

Having been in business for more than two decades, I have learned much when it comes to hiring. Let me share:

1. If you are working solo in your startup, as soon as you are ready to expand your staff the first person to hire is your assistant, to help take some of the administrative load off of you. This will free up time for you to focus on the more important things.

2. The second person to hire is the most important key executive who can help you build the company and hire the remaining leadership team. You have to start from the C-suite and then develop the staffing plan all the way down. Who this person is may depend on what new competencies you need to complement your own or to supplement what you cannot do.

3. Anyone you hire must be able to lead right now. Do not hire for future potential, but rather for immediate results.

4. Avoid using recruiting companies to do your hiring. Early-stage startups usually cannot afford recruiting firms anyway, but more importantly, it is highly useful for founders to identify on their own

the talent they need. When I hired the key executives for Sunstone Management, Sunstone Trust Company, and Partake Collective, I took months, even years, to get to know the executives I ended up hiring. For Sunstone Management, I served as CEO for seven years as I sized up various individuals and decided that John Keisler had the right talent to become its CEO. I brought Dan Wheeler into Sunstone Trust Company first as interim CEO and challenged him to take us through the regulatory application before making him permanent CEO. I worked closely with and observed first-hand Adam Carrillo's expertise before offering him the VP position in Sunstone Management to work with me on establishing Partake Collective. Patience is the key to ensuring you will feel comfortable when you make an offer to someone to join your executive team.

5. Keep perfecting your vision statement at every interview until you are confident it is emotionally moving and intellectually persuasive. Your vision statement is your primary weapon in hiring exceptional talent in a competitive world.

6. If your best candidate lives far away and asks to be compensated for the expenses of moving, my experience has been that it is always worthwhile to pay those expenses if the candidate truly appreciates the vision statement.

STRATEGIES FOR RETAINING GREAT EMPLOYEES: TREAT PEOPLE WELL

Here is what I have learned about how to inspire loyalty and keep your employees for years.

1. Given that my leadership style is of the "servant leader" type, I believe in treating people well and encouraging them to work hard. Good leaders always treat people with respect and courtesy. Being nice also includes treating everyone equally, without favor. Whether the person is an executive or a novice employee, good leaders treat them the way every human being deserves to be treated.

2. When you make people feel appreciated, they are comfortable being around you. This builds mutual trust. And when there is trust, people are less defensive and less motivated to be argumentative while sharing a differing opinion with you and others. Their ego is not threatened when they know you respect them. This shared comfort improves discussions, brainstorming sessions, and even times when you might need to offer criticism to someone about their performance.

3. While your company is small, treat employees as if you are all family. This means creating a company culture of friendliness, non-competitiveness, transparency, and mutual affirmation of everyone's importance, no matter the level of their position. A company with such a familial culture celebrates victories together, which can even include going out after business hours for meals and drinks, at the company's expense.

4. As your company grows beyond 20 or 30 people, it becomes more difficult to continue the feeling of being family. There are simply too many people and it becomes harder to maintain the same closeness to everyone. Smaller family segments may form within the company. The key now is to avoid internal rivalries for attention and resources. Continue being as transparent with all employees as possible.

5. Beyond 20 or 30 employees, you likely need to introduce more hierarchy and a layer of management. You alone cannot lead such a large staff. The number of managers you will need depends on your size and industry. You might need one general manager and several sub-managers.

6. A common rule of thumb is that a single manager can manage seven or eight people and still have time to do his or her own work. Beyond that number, it is unlikely the manager will accomplish any work of their own. The trend in today's corporate world is for flatter hierarchies, with only one or two layers of management between the lowest level employee and the CEO.

Interview with Chingy Norton,
ALC Employee

What is it like to work at ALC?

Chingy Norton

I started with ALC in 2012, so I was among the very first employees in the company. We were a new company at that time, and John Shen treated us much like a family. We often had group potluck lunches (and John would even make food at home to bring in to share at the lunch table). Sometimes we would all go out on Friday nights for drinks and karaoke singing. I did a lot of work for Stella at that time, as John was often traveling to China to secure EB-5 investors.

Our employee count has expanded a lot since then so we obviously can no longer have communal lunches. Besides, nowadays, a lot of employees order takeout and get it delivered (which is actually really good proof of John's concept of ghost kitchens that reflects his launching of Partake Collective).

I think how we employees were treated in the early years of the company explains a lot about why we are so successful. I like to say that people enjoy working with other people whom they would actually have dinner with. If you would not eat a meal with someone, you would not work with them. The point is, most of the employees in this company have been here for years; they are loyal, enjoy their work and love working for John and the other executives. Before we moved to Irvine, I used to drive 26 miles to Long Beach and 26 miles back home but it didn't bother me because I loved doing my job so much. The company is essentially my second home. I even bring my son to work sometimes; he sits in John's office watching the fish in the aquarium, while John is at his desk working, unfazed by having my son in his office.

In the 10 years I have been with ALC, I have seen the company go through many changes and growth spurts. John has been an inspiring leader for everyone. He has an open door policy and anyone can get time to speak to him. One of most difficult times we had was when we got authorized to do the PPP loans that the government program created to help small businesses during Covid. We were inundated with loan applications and we worked day and night to get the paperwork done. Everyone was pitching in, staying very late at night and working weekends. But it was not just the employees; our leaders were right there working alongside us.

One great advantage of working in a fast-growing entrepreneurial company is that you always learn a lot. In my ten years here, I have learned so much about each of the new businesses that John created and also from all the new people we have had to hire. Every one of them can offer us something new to learn.

Dealing with Mistakes, Failures, and Firing Employees

There is a trend in the business literature suggesting that leaders are supposed to allow, even encourage, people to make mistakes and to fail. In Silicon Valley, mistakes and failure are practically badges of courage, proving that you were willing to take risks and go for the brass ring. In this philosophy, leaders must look past mistakes and appreciate the effort that people have put into just trying. They learned something from their mistake, so they might have a better chance at success next time.

My response is: nonsense. This attitude is simply a good excuse to justify that people make mistakes and you cannot stop them from doing so. In my view, this is counterproductive. No entrepreneur wants to encourage mistakes by employees or turn a blind eye to them. One may not be able to stop them, but you cannot give people the impression that you *welcome* mistakes. Mistakes cause damage. I am sure that if an entrepreneur could pull a lever to shut down all employee mistakes, they would do so.

No entrepreneur
wants to encourage mistakes
by employees or turn
a blind eye to them.
One may not be able to stop
them, but you cannot
give people the impression
that you *welcome* mistakes.
Mistakes cause damage.

If someone commits a mistake once, yes, you might look past it. But committing the same mistake two or more times—or constantly making different mistakes—means something is wrong. The person either needs more training or is simply not the right fit for your organization.

I have experienced my share of employee mistakes over the past decade. The worst was an employee who approved an EB-5 investment for a family in China without following the EB-5 rules against investing in businesses with certain unauthorized industry codes. The wrong industry code completely negated this investment, which meant that the family's money was invested in a business that would not allow them to obtain their immigration status. We could not withdraw the investment and the family would face a denial of its immigration petitions. Mistakes like this damage your company and so this employee could no longer be entitled to have such responsibility. I let him go.

The idea of allowing people to take risks under the rubric of "experimentation" is equally suspect. In my three financial businesses we take risks every day, some of them quite large. Not a single day goes by where we do not take risks. And I love it. I am willing to let my co-workers take risks as well.

But our risk-taking does not mean I believe in experimentation. The term "experiment" itself suggests that you don't know much about the prospects of success. Before we commit to any risk, we have tools to assess the probability of a positive outcome. We study the people involved, the project, and the monetary investment. By the time we decide to take that risk, it is a sound business decision, not an experiment.

The fact is, you can't avoid risks, but you have to challenge yourself to survive them. You don't want to look back and say a given risk was actually a mistake and you should have known better.

Firing People Is Often the Right Decision

Releasing people—aka, firing them—is a necessary part of life as an entrepreneur. It is irresponsible to your business to assume you will never fire someone or to believe that you do not have the right to let an employee go.

As a leader, you need to think about not just the job performance and feelings of the person you may need to fire, but the impact that this person has on the other members of your team. One person's poor performance or inability to fit into your company culture can drag your results downwards. Sometimes you have to make a decision to let someone go because they make too many mistakes; other times, they have a pattern of poor performance; and still other times, the skills you hired them for are not as strong as you expected. When you fire someone for any of these reasons, you are being a smart entrepreneur.

My style in firing someone is to display courtesy to the person and find a way to help them save their self-esteem. The worst scenario is that you let people go and they decide to retaliate by suing you. My experience, and that of other entrepreneurs I have spoken to, is that such lawsuits occur most often not because the person disputes your reason for firing them, but because of how they were treated when fired. Any type of public humiliation or denigration can become cause for a winning lawsuit. People will fight for their self-esteem. Even if you win the case in court against the plaintiff, the legal fees and time still cost you and set you back.

My style in firing someone is to display courtesy to the person and find a way to help them save their self-esteem.

Leading Your Companies Through Growing Pains

Growing one company is like gardening a backyard plot. Growing multiple companies is like farming 10 acres of land producing 20 types of vegetables. You are going to be a lot busier than you can possibly imagine, but that is the excitement and joy of being a parallel entrepreneur.

Every startup will experience barriers and roadblocks, and your job as leader is to keep the company on an even keel as you navigate through them. You will face challenges of all sorts on a nearly daily basis. It may feel like the game of whack-a-mole, solving a problem in one company one day, but then another problem pops up in another of your companies the next day. It may seem as if you have no respite from being the leader.

There are two important observations I want to share based on my experience. First, as you grow your startup, your workload and activity are going to increase. You may find it difficult to hire fast enough. If you are operating multiple companies, try to leverage your staff among the companies and have them share jobs. For example, we share the CFO for Sunstone Management with Partake Collective. She works on behalf of both companies. At a certain point, Partake Collective will need its own CFO, but initially, leveraging her skills for these dual functions has worked well.

Every startup will experience barriers and roadblocks, and your job as leader is to keep the company on an even keel as you navigate through them. You will face challenges of all sorts on a nearly daily basis. It may feel like the game of whack-a-mole, solving a problem in one company one day, but then another problem pops up in another of your companies the next day.

Second, there is a risk to be aware of when you grow very quickly: employees may begin to experience frustration and even burnout with their work. Their prior stellar performance may suffer. Such symptoms often appear when a company is growing very fast. Startups that succeed very quickly often cannot hire fast enough and so they ask employees to adapt to new processes and procedures, or even to take on extra job functions. Employees may find themselves challenged to do more than they were hired to do—but they cannot adapt to the new roles, hard as they try. Remember, not all employees can learn to do new things at the same speed as others.

Fast growth can be especially hard on employees who do not have an entrepreneurial mentality. Be careful about giving such employees poor performance reviews or threatening to fire them if the reality is that they simply cannot keep up with your growth. There may be other solutions to retain them if their former performance was acceptable or excellent. Such employees may remain loyal to you if they had a different job position.

A final issue to watch for as you grow is that some of your key executives may begin to feel they are deserving of greater rewards for having led the family, such as stock options or a share in the company ownership. That is fine, if you are read to offer such perks. Stock options are popular in the tech world because there is great potential value if the company goes public.

But many non-tech startups are too small and stock options do not make sense. These companies are not like law firms where executives can earn their way to becoming a partner and sharing in the profits. In short, you need to plan for the day when your company or multiple companies are ready to have stock options or other financial rewards for key players.

HR and IT Departments

OUTSOURCING VS. HIRING

It makes perfect sense that startups do not need an HR department at the beginning of their journey. If you are the CEO and sole employee of your startup and need to hire an assistant, you can create your own employment contract using online templates. Even hiring your first executive might be done using templated employment contracts.

However, once you have gotten to the point of having ten employees, it might be smart to engage an external Human Resource company to take over your employment contracts and policies, benefit packages, and payroll. These administrative tasks are too complex and detailed for you to manage, given your other priority leadership responsibilities. An outside HR department is a necessary expense that will prove its value to you as you grow.

With further growth, you will eventually benefit by bringing the HR function inside the company. In fact, there is a common formula that says once you have 34 employees, an internal HR department makes sense given the number of people and variety of positions your company has.

If you are a parallel entrepreneur with multiple companies, you can leverage the HR tasks by having one single HR department that oversees all of your sister companies. There is a benefit to this: equality of treatment. In my experience, employees in your companies will share information about their salaries and benefits, even if your companies are in very different industries. An HR professional can help you determine what would be considered equal salaries, benefits, and perks across your companies.

If you are a parallel entrepreneur with multiple companies, you can leverage the HR tasks by having one single HR department that oversees all of your sister companies. There is a benefit to this: equality of treatment.

There is a similar pattern to your IT needs. In the beginning, you may need to hire an external IT consultant to manage your IT needs. If you are a tech startup, you might have had the IT professional(s) on your staff in the early startup stages; but, just as with HR, at some point you may grow large enough that it would be beneficial to hire an external company to manage all your IT affairs. Then, when you reach 25 or 30 employees, you might want to bring in your own IT professional(s) to create an internal IT department that can be more efficient and responsive to your IT needs.

Leading your company through growing pains is a substantial challenge for an entrepreneur with one company. Being successful at growing two, three, or more companies is daunting, but it can be done. Don't give up early as you begin to experience these growing pains. They will feel overwhelming at first, but like anything you need to master, it takes time to learn to juggle the challenges and bat down the moles that keep popping up.

The Benefits of Having a Board of Directors and Advisory Committees

Startup success depends on a combination of many components of leadership within a company. One critical component includes the development of a strong board of directors and/or an advisory committee. An advisory committee provides advice and guidance on long-term planning and strategic planning, while a board of directors is responsible for governance of the company's operations.

For most startups, forming and managing a board of directors or even just an advisory committee can be a challenge. Many founders in the early stage of their startup may not fully appreciate the value of these complementary leadership roles. They typically think they must stay laser-focused on the development of their products or services without any distractions or slowdowns caused by expanded discussions and debates. In addition to this mindset, startup owners may also struggle to build a strong relationship with perfect candidates, especially well-accomplished business leaders, for either the board of directors or an advisory committee. Without such a relationship and good personal trust, no matter how attractive the business concept sounds, successful professionals may not easily accept the invitation to serve as a director or advisor.

I believe the sooner an entrepreneur establishes a solid board and more importantly, a business development-oriented advisory committee, the greater the chances of achieving long-term success.

The sooner an entrepreneur establishes a solid board and more importantly, a business development-oriented advisory committee, the greater the chances of achieving long-term success.

I had not recognized the value of these external groups until early 2020 when Covid-19 hit. Although I had a board of directors in prior years for American Lending Center, I had not consulted with them very deeply to explore how they could help me. The reason? My board included only three shareholders who also happened to be management team members, so there was no need to discuss at board meetings the same issues the management team was already discussing. Therefore, we held no regular board meetings.

When the Covid crisis arrived, I faced a lot of pressure to look for quick solutions, otherwise ALC's business might die in a few months. I was forced to look around and discuss our options with smart and experienced external professionals in my network. I put together a small group of advisors to help us regain our footing—and since then we have continued regular meetings focused on ongoing business development. This advisory group has made my job as CEO a lot easier.

I highly recommend every startup initially build, at the minimum, an advisory committee, and once the company has grown large enough (and profitable enough), eventually work towards forming a functional, professional board of directors. If you are not able to hire heavyweights for such a board, but want to get external stakeholders engaged, the best action to take is to invite them to join an advisory committee. Their voices can then be heard, their ideas can shine, and there are only minimal costs to make that happen.

Here are my recommendations for how to work with each type of leadership complement.

ADVISORY COMMITTEE

An advisory committee can be a first step for a startup to bring in external experience and expertise. The advantage of an advisory committee is that the members do not have governing power or any legal fiduciary responsibility as do the members of a board of directors. They cannot issue directives to executives or employees that must be followed.

Advisors are also selected solely by the CEO or company founder, not elected by shareholders. Their purpose is solely to provide expert opinions and feedback to the founder(s) regarding issues such as trends, market strategy, and competitive analysis. Given the distinctions, advisory board members must be careful not to act like board directors because, should a loss of profits occur, shareholders can sue them if it appears that at some time they participated in governing the company.

Advisory boards may meet each quarter to discuss strategic progress and report on any new trends or technologies that the members know about, given their fields of expertise. The committee can also play an important public relations role, serving in part as an advocate for the company in the market, gathering input from relevant constituencies, and providing feedback to the founders.

It can be beneficial to create an advisory committee during the early stages of developing a program so that committee members can provide advice concerning the design and plans for the company. It is easiest to begin with a small advisory committee, for example, four to seven community leaders and/or industry experts, during the planning process. While advisory committees cannot create legally binding policies for the organization, they can help create policies that provide direction and support for the program staff.

Note that advisory committees often have fixed terms of service where members are appointed to a specific term. Advisory committees benefit from having clear policies and responsibilities like those of a governing board of directors, e.g., meeting attendance, decision-making, and ethics policies. A charter and a written description of the role and responsibility of advisory committee members is thus critical.

BOARD OF DIRECTORS

Private companies are not required to have independent members on a board of directors. However, given the pace and scope of change in today's environment, a board of directors collectively—as well as each member individually—can play a critical role in the overall success of a startup once it has grown large enough to warrant having one or when the company goes public. In general, the shareholders of the company vote to appoint board members.

> # A board of directors collectively—as well as each member individually—can play a critical role in the overall success of a startup once it has grown large enough to warrant having one or when the company goes public.

In young startups, the CEO has the final say in all corporate matters and may also be chair of the board, though the chair can be another board member. In conjunction with the CEO, board directors are responsible for establishing and maintaining the company's corporate governance framework. Definitions of corporate governance vary, but they typically focus on the company's relationships, policies, and processes that provide strategic direction and controls. Strong corporate governance is the foundation for safe and sound operations. The board must ensure that the company's affairs are carried out in compliance with applicable laws, competently, and ethically. The board

John Shen

should ensure that all major operational areas and activities are covered by clearly communicated policies that can be readily understood by all employees.

Board members do not need to be experts in the industry of your startup, but it is their diversity of business experience, education, and opinions that makes them valuable to you. When selecting potential board members, you therefore want to seek people who can complement your skills and those of your executive team. You might even map out the expertise you need to fulfill your mission. Another objective is to establish a lineup of directors that is more reflective of the texture of wider societal changes.

Boards must meet at least once per year, but in larger organizations, they typically meet at least quarterly. Meetings should have a clear agenda, with notes taken and minutes kept for legal purposes. Most organizations pay board members either an annual retainer or at least a per meeting fee. Be sure to consult your legal counsel for details on forming a board of directors.

The Three Phases of Leadership for a Parallel Entrepreneur

To close this chapter, let me add one thought. Being a parallel entrepreneur requires you to think of your formal leadership titles in a different way. When you own and operate a single company, you are likely to have the title of CEO. But as you grow that first company and expand into owning a second or third company, you need to think carefully about how many of those companies require you to be the actual CEO, especially if you eventually become chair of the board.

When I began my startup Sunstone Management, I kept the title of CEO for seven years in addition to my CEO role in ALC. But as soon

The three phases of becoming a parallel entrepreneur

as I started Sunstone Trust Company, I yielded that CEO position and I hired an interim CEO who later became the permanent CEO. Similarly, with Partake Collective, I brought in a leader and made him a VP at Sunstone Management in charge of Partake Collective, and then later made him full-time CEO of Partake Collective.

The point is, there are many ways to assign official titles to yourself and your key executives as you build your startup ventures and transform them into sustainable companies. What I consider the overriding principle of entrepreneurial leadership is that you must mature with your companies. Your leadership capacity will develop and mature as you launch additional companies. Over time, you will need to step back further and further to have a wider view of each company's future. I think of the leadership process for a parallel entrepreneur as occurring in phases:

- *Your Entrepreneurship 1.0 phase:* This is when you first launch your venture; here, you are simply an entrepreneur. You have hardly any staff, so even if you call yourself CEO, you are captain of a small boat. That is plenty of responsibility in the beginning. If it is your first startup, you will face enormous challenges as CEO.

- *Your Entrepreneurship 2.0 phase:* This is when your first company is gaining in success and you may be thinking about launching another firm. You are now much more of a formal CEO. Your leadership is more about organizational management, shepherding your first company to greater revenue and profit.

- *Your Entrepreneurship 3.0 phase:* This is when you begin launching a second company and perhaps a third or more. You are entering the world of a true parallel entrepreneur at this point. The reality now is that you can no longer remain as CEO of several companies. You might remain the CEO of one company that requires the least amount of your time, but you need to promote yourself to chairman of the board of all your companies. This transformation gives you the time and impetus to widen your vision so you can focus on identifying opportunities for your companies.

FIRST-GENERATION ENTREPRENEURS: SPECIAL ISSUES REGARDING LEADERSHIP

First-generation immigrants who are entrepreneurs may or may not struggle with leadership. For those who are like me in their personality and cultural background, there can be a plethora of reasons that leadership does not come naturally to you. You may have been raised to be quiet, unassuming, and the exact opposite of authoritative or boss-like. You may come from a country where the culture expects people to follow, not lead.

In Chinese culture, for example, we have thousands of years of history of dictatorial authoritarianism. Chinese people do what they are told to do. Our culture trains us to follow instructions and not ask questions. The Chinese population is, in many ways, the very definition of a subservient employee culture. In addition, China and other Asian countries have large populations that believe in Taoism. This is a spiritual belief system that values peaceful, calm existence. Everyone needs to be respectful and conservative in their manners. When a Chinese person emigrates to the US, he or she brings this cultural mindset along.

Some immigrants to the US come from European nations, each of which has its own cultural legacy. People from Scandinavian countries such as Denmark may adhere to the "Law of Jante," a tacit code of conduct that dictates that no one is better than anyone else and that it is improper to do something that is for personal ambition. People from Sweden often believe that decisions are best made by groups, so leadership in their view is an egalitarian, collaborative effort. Immigrants from many European, South American, African, and Asian countries may bring inherently different leadership styles, as well. These can be misinterpreted by some Americans, who then will not follow their leader.

Understanding your own cultural heritage and how it may impact your leadership style is thus a big challenge for many first-generation entrepreneurs. For some, it can be extremely challenging to adapt to the American style of business where leaders can seem aggressive, bossy, antagonistic, or authoritarian—yet it may be necessary to act that way in order to achieve success. For example, a first-generation Asian-born entrepreneur will find it very difficult to adopt these types of behaviors.

Self-awareness is an important starting point to becoming a great leader and parallel entrepreneur. If you can identify what leadership qualities you may be lacking, due to your cultural background and your individual personality, and then make an effort to bring them into your life, you can learn to become a good leader. Through practice, you can modify your persona and still feel authentic about who you are. Just as I did, you can make an intentional effort to master the qualities of exceptional leadership, which I consider to be: a visionary outlook, respect for your employees, thoughtful decision-making, fairness to everyone, and a dab of charisma and dynamism to inspire others.

For me, perhaps the single most important key to leadership is being able to communicate clearly. You need to be able to deliver the right message at the right time in the right format. If you are not able to do that, you are unlikely to achieve the status of being a great leader. This is a quality that you can master through practice and effort.

For instance, when I was working in Kalamazoo after I got out of graduate school, I wanted to focus on work and I didn't want to spend time learning about the other people in my sphere. I was still shy and inwardly focused. I did not make efforts to develop a network of friends and personal contacts. Then I realized it was a problem for me: I could not be part of a team at work as I found it difficult to relate to others.

So I decided that I would make an effort to change myself. I started by talking to another programmer who was American. I consciously pushed myself to open up and spend time after work to hang out with him and other colleagues. I went to his home and spent time with his lovely family several days a week. We became friends and I played games and had dinners with them. This experience helped me become more friendly and gradually I was able to change myself and become a more communicative person. I am a very different person than who I used to be ten years ago, and even more so from the person I was five decades ago growing up in China.

John Shen

REFLECTIONS

Consider these questions. Write out your answers or identify a "success buddy" such as a business partner, another entrepreneur, or a spouse or friend with whom you can discuss the questions.

- What style of leadership are you naturally inclined to? Are you self-confident, extroverted, loquacious, and commanding? Or are you more introverted, interested in encouraging and listening to others, and finding agreement through consensus? And ask yourself, what type of leadership does your enterprise need?

- What type of leader do you want to be? What capabilities are you lacking to be a great leader as you define it?

- Are you acting as a visionary in your company? Can you see trends in your industry shaping up that offer you opportunities to grow your company or launch a new one?

- What is your approach to hiring people? Have you been successful in identifying and hiring the top talents you need?

- Do you have difficulty providing critical feedback to your staff?

- Do you need to fire anyone? Do you hesitate to do it? Are there alternatives to letting that individual go?

CHAPTER 8

Balance

BALANCE

- From Latin *bi-* meaning two and *-lanx*, meaning a scale pan. Balance is having two scale pans that even out in the weight each one holds.

- Synonyms: equilibrium, stability

John Shen

Life as an entrepreneur is beyond challenging, to say the least. Given your strong drive and ambition to succeed, and the constant need to work, watch trends, and identify opportunities, it will feel like you must devote every waking hour of every day to your company. And if you are a parallel entrepreneur, the drive to make every company you own succeed will multiply those pressures. You might think that a parallel entrepreneur should never enjoy a relaxing day with the family, take a vacation, or just sleep late on Sunday.

Many entrepreneurs claim that their work is so much fun they do not have an issue with feeling stressed. That may be true. But let me be the first to persuade you that the entrepreneur's life cannot be all work, no matter how much fun it is. You need a BALANCE between work and life. Learning to create this balance is the final talent of a smart entrepreneur, especially if you are a parallel one. In this chapter I want to share my principles of Balance.

My Journey to Living with Balance

It has taken me more than two decades to arrive at a sense of balance in my entrepreneurial life. When you first start out as an entrepreneur, it feels nearly impossible to stop working day and night. Your hours at the office blend seamlessly into your personal time at home. You constantly think about business, answering calls and emails, meeting people, or drafting something of importance for the company.

When I began my real estate business in Florida, I also had a full-time job in Philadelphia. Every weekend, I flew around the country giving presentations about how lucrative it was to buy property in the Orlando area. I was gone from Friday night to Monday morning, then worked long hours at my job during the week. I hardly saw my family.

When I left that job and moved my family to Florida so I could spend 100% of my time growing my real estate businesses, my family life worsened. My wife and I began having serious problems that eventually led to a separation for many years. We lived in different houses and spent separate time with our children. When the real estate market crashed in 2007, along with my business in 2008, we were so estranged that we agreed to divorce. Like many couples, we had irreconcilable differences in our philosophy and approach to daily life. But the relatively non-stop drive I had to grow my businesses in Florida was a significant factor contributing to our conflicted family dynamics.

Later, when I launched ALC after the period of losing my real estate business, it was easy to go back to working nearly 24/7. Being divorced, all my time was my own; nothing interfered with my drive to succeed. I took pleasure from working all the time and believed that success was the only objective that created meaning in my life. I had failed in business once before and I was committed to succeeding this time around. And since I was launching a new company, I had no employees, just a couple of partners. Each of us had to cover every task and every job. For me, there was also much frequent international traveling too. Although I was doing something I myself had chosen to do, I had no time for "life."

Since 2010, I have been slowly learning to adopt a philosophy of balance in how I apportion my time, focus, and energy between work and my personal life. I do not want a repeat of my past experience and divorce. My past decade of reflecting on living with balance has left me with nine principles to share with every entrepreneur—and especially if you intend to be a parallel entrepreneur.

9 BALANCE PRINCIPLES

1.

By neglecting your life, you will have no life that makes work worthwhile.

2.

To be an entrepreneur, you need a partner willing to make the journey with you.

3.

Rise early, exercise, and eat for health.

4.

Prioritize your tasks and calendar your time.

5.

Don't let meetings dominate your work time.

6.

Control your addiction to your phone.

7.

Know when to end your day.

8.

Develop habits and routines to manage stress.

9.

Give back to society.

BALANCE PRINCIPLE 1

By neglecting your life, you will have no life that makes work worthwhile.

I do not believe in success just for the sake of wealth, prestige, perks, or the admiration of others. For me, those are not the richest part of life. Yes, you need to work many hours a week when you are an entrepreneur, but I have learned that much of what you perceive as important is not as important as your personal life and your family.

The drive to succeed is a powerful, brutal force. It can feel impossible to turn it off, so you need to learn how to balance it with an equally strong drive to remain healthy and psychologically happy. If you believe that the only feeling that makes you happy is what you feel when you work, you are on a path to unhappiness.

The drive to succeed is a powerful, brutal force.
It can feel impossible to turn it off, so you need to learn how to balance it with an equally strong drive to remain healthy and psychologically happy.

John Shen

To bring balance into your life, spend time figuring out what you can give up doing so that you don't sacrifice your family or the fun of living. The biggest mistake you can make is to treat everything as less important than work. You might think you need to spend every single minute building your business, but if you lose those people you love dearly, you have lost your most precious legacy. The damage especially from losing your family can be huge. The psychological toll it can take on you has far-reaching ramifications. It can be an enormous distraction from your work and even result in bad decisions that make you drive your business into failure rather than success.

BALANCE PRINCIPLE 2

To be an entrepreneur, you need a partner willing to make the journey with you.

If you are not married yet, be careful in your choice of partner. Having a partner or spouse who does not understand the level of commitment you want to give your company will add a layer of complexity to your life that you do not need and cannot afford. Neither of you desires to spend your precious hours in conflict over how much time you devote to company business. No marriage is happy or blossoms when there are resentments about missed time together or feelings of neglect. Meanwhile, a spouse who consistently protests against your commitment to work and your drive to succeed is effectively failing to appreciate your inner entrepreneurial spirit.

If you are already married and experiencing difficulties, it is important to begin talking openly about your situation. Professional couples counseling can help unravel complex issues and lead you both to a shared understanding about how you can balance your business with your relationship or marriage. Being an entrepreneur demands sacrifices from both of you and you may need to do some negotiating. In the end, remember that divorce can be very painful and take a toll on your entrepreneurial spirit as well.

WORKING WITH YOUR SPOUSE

If you are one-half of a couple that works together in an entre-preneurial venture, whether as co-founders or with one of you as CEO while the other is an employee, I have rec-ommendations for you based on personal experience. My wife, Stella, and I have been working together for nearly a decade. Stella serves as Chief

Stella Zhang and John Shen

Operating Officer of ALC, while I am its CEO as well as chairman of the board for all my companies. Stella is now also a partner with me in all of them.

Whether you are working as your spouse's co-equal or one of you is the boss of the other, both situations require constant sensitivity to your dynamics to keep your lives in balance. You must respect each other according to the line of authority you create in your work capac-ity while nevertheless honoring each other as equal spouses in your home life. This can be difficult to do, and mistakes are easy.

The spouse with more authority at work may accidentally bring that persona home, failing to distinguish the line between work and home life. Like a metaphorical prenuptial agreement, it can help that you talk honestly about your feelings in working together, then fashion a clear understanding of boundaries to preserve your marriage and work relationship. I believe that employees should know you are mar-ried but should not be witness to your marital disputes. Never argue from your marital persona when at work. If you disagree when you are in meetings together, do not drop back into your marriage roles.

One of the most difficult lines to draw for couples working together is how much business and what part of the business to discuss at home. Over our years working together, Stella and I have passed through several phases of limitations and we have now landed on perhaps what is the best one. Years ago, we used to talk extensively about work when we were home. With both of us involved in ALC, many dinner conversations and weekend outings became extensions of our business day. It felt like we could not stop talking about work, there were so many challenges and issues we both wanted to share. We each believed that it was healthy to seek out the other's opinion on problems, and sometimes this led to debates and arguments.

After a while, we both recognized that this limitless approach was unhealthy. We were overwhelmed with business talk and could no longer see the forest for the trees of our home life. It was a problem for my children too. Despite the business pressures we faced in growing the companies I had founded in my Entrepreneurship 2.0 phase, we agreed to put a boundary on talking about work when at home. Our decision: we can talk about a business matter "in general" for a brief time at night or on weekends, but we would not get mired in its details. I also proposed that we'd only touch the "happy" part of the business after the work hours. If the conversation veered into too much detail or touched on a painful part of the business, we consciously curtailed talking. It was like a chemistry we shared, knowing when to halt our dialogue.

This worked for a while, but then we both came to realize it was an artificial and unproductive strategy. We were forsaking the benefits of being a couple working together who had extra time to discuss some issues in depth at home. Some topics were worthy of conversation after hours. The philosophy that we abide by today is not to create a false sense of boundaries. We have to give ourselves the flexibility to discuss certain issues no matter when or where. However, we also are aware that we cannot let work take over our home life. You need to reserve time at home to talk about "normal" topics—the neighborhood, the kids' activities, the trash pickup, the mail, household maintenance, the grocery store shopping list—and for fun with the family. These are all the things that make up a high quality of life.

Interview with Stella Zhang

How did you arrive at working with John and what is it like being spouses who work together?

Stella Zhang

My life trajectory is slightly different than John's, though it may be equally surprising and inspiring for some readers. I was born in China and stayed there through my university years. I graduated with a master's degree in English. I then worked for a company that in 1997 had a business trip to the US, which I went on. During that trip, there were some changes that occurred in the company and I decided to stay in the States.

I ended up getting a job with an immigration law firm in Orange County and worked there for 14 years. Through that experience I learned a lot about immigration law and how to take care of our firm's clients. During my time at the firm, I also decided I wanted to get an MBA, so I applied and got accepted to the University of California, Irvine. I attended classes at night and earned my degree in 2005.

I met John just as he was starting American Lending Center and his new EB-5 business. He asked me to join his company given my business background and knowledge of immigration law. We eventually married and that's how we ended up as spouses working together for more than a decade now. Perhaps one thing that makes it easy for us is that we were not young college graduates starting a business together. We were always in it for the long term and so we had the patience necessary to work hard and make our dream come true. The many hours we put into

272

the work does not make us feel deprived of other things in life. I am proud to have contributed to making our businesses grow so much. In fact, working together has brought us closer. We try not to talk too much about work at home, especially with our older parents at home. You try to be a problem solver and not a troublemaker. It's a different kind of feeling of happiness.

As COO of American Lending Center, what are your expectations for the business?

In ALC, we have two functions: 1) helping our investors qualify for and get their green cards, and 2) making sure they make good investments. We work closely with our investors to form different entities that can provide them with financial returns and the opportunity to live in the US. One of the keys to ALC is the development of trust with our clients. There has been a lot of abuse and fraud in the EB-5 program, especially in its early years. Many EB-5 agents took the money, exaggerated the costs of the project and kept much of the profits. Or they invested in bad projects that did not deliver.

When we entered the business we were like a baby compared to the big EB-5 firms. It took a lot of hard work. I was and still am very involved in every detail. We focus on construction projects that cost a lot of money. We typically work with other lenders who are the originating loan party; most of these are capital firms. When they have a loan they want to split up to reduce their risk, they come to us to co-fund it with them, which helps them get the funds faster and it reduces their risk. These loans usually have a payback period of five to seven years.

What is the startup sponsorship that you provide to UC Irvine?

When we decided to move from Long Beach to Irvine in 2020, we started to contact people to begin making connections with this community that we wanted to become an integral part of. We heard that UC Irvine, my alma mater for my MBA, had a startup pitch competition for students, faculty, and alumni. They called it New Ventures and they were seeking donors to help fund the awards prizes.

Given our passion for startups and our work with the Long Beach Accelerator and Cal State Long Beach pitch competition, I spoke with one of the professors involved (who happened to have been one of my MBA professors), and I offered to fund the competition. I was honored when they named it after me, the Stella Zhang New Venture Competition. I am not used to being under the spotlight, but I am thrilled to be part of it. The most recent competition awards night occurred in June 2022, where we awarded $100,000 in prizes to a number of winning teams across five tracks, including a Grand Prize of $20,000.

We also are now sponsoring an event called Born in California, which is a demo day for startups coming from the entire University of California system. And most exciting, we are looking into developing a UCI Accelerator using the same model that John used with the Long Beach Accelerator. We want to create it as a three-way partnership with the school, the City of Irvine, and Sunstone Management. Eventually, we see ourselves working to copy this accelerator concept to establish many three-party partnerships with other schools in cities across the US.

BALANCE PRINCIPLE 3

Rise early, exercise, and eat for health.

With the stress of being an entrepreneur, you can become unhealthy very easily. The pressure to constantly work and produce results makes it tempting to avoid anything that takes time and focus away from your job. You need to combat this by developing habits that keep you healthy and energized.

Keeping yourself in shape means that you eat healthy, sleep well, and give yourself a chance to work out or exercise daily, even if it is just walking. You have to do at least

Keeping yourself in shape means that you eat healthy, sleep well, and give yourself a chance to work out or exercise daily, even if it is just walking. You have to do at least something to stay fit because when you are physically in shape, you have more energy. Taking one hour away from your company to exercise may mean you lose an hour of work, but your overall efficiency will be higher.

something to stay fit because when you are physically in shape, you have more energy. Taking one hour away from your company to exercise may mean you lose an hour of work, but your overall efficiency will be higher.

I work out every day. I get up at 5:30 or 6:00 a.m. and exercise for an hour at a gym in my office building. I then take a shower and get ready for work, feeling invigorated from the workout. I eat a light breakfast, such as a couple of eggs and a yogurt, so that I do not feel weighted down by a heavy meal in my stomach when I start my day. I am in my office by 8:30 each morning, ready to tackle the urgent issues of the day.

I also make time for lunch every day. I have learned that eating quickly at your desk is a habit that leads to becoming unhealthy. Rather than saving time, it feeds your stress level, as your mind is focused on your work, not on enjoying your meal or the people with whom you might be lunching. It is far healthier to have a casual business lunch; and aim to spend some of that time talking about life in general, not just business.

BALANCE PRINCIPLE 4

Prioritize your tasks and calendar your time.

The key for any entrepreneur, but especially parallel entrepreneurs, is figuring out how to manage time. Your hours are filled with tasks that feel like they must be completed, often many more tasks than you can possibly fit into a day. It can be very disconcerting when you discover that many of these tasks appear to need to get done simultaneously, as if they have the same deadline. It should therefore not come as news that the smart entrepreneur must use a calendar system or, at minimum, a list that prioritizes your tasks, especially if you do not have an assistant doing it for you.

Each morning when I arrive at my desk, I review the daily list of to-dos that I left myself the night before. I normally divide the to-dos on my list into just three categories in terms of priority levels: Urgent, Priority #1, and Priority #2. As soon as I finish one, I pull out the to-do list and delete that completed one. When I need to add a new to-do, I immediately pick a proper priority level and add it to the list. Sometimes, due to a deadline change, I may also re-prioritize some of the existing to-dos. Every single workday I keep practicing this. This system is simple enough for me to maintain, even owning mulitple companies.

Urgent	Priority 1	Priority 2

Whatever system you have, at any moment during the work hours you must be able to see a clear set of prioritized and targeted tasks to complete. Should you need to update something, such as adding a new task, removing a task, or making a priority level change on any task, be sure to put it on your calendar. This is a sort of "firefighter" approach to getting the most urgent work done first, be it scheduled work or a sudden "fire" that needs to be put out. But such shuffling of tasks is what allows you to keep up with the fast and subtle changes in the work.

Finally, be honest with yourself about your calendar. You know there are some tasks you simply do not want to do. Rather than to procrastinate doing them, rationalizing some false reason they are not getting done, just admit to yourself, "I don't want to do this, but I must." Then do it.

The MVP in Many Companies is Your Assistant

As soon as you can afford to hire an employee, it should be an assistant dedicated first to your needs. The value of having a smart, proactive, forward-thinking assistant cannot be overestimated. The right person can save hours of time per day, increasing your efficiency and productivity. The assistant should be in charge of your calendar or task list, remind you of appointments, set up meetings and Zoom sessions, manage the office's operations, and in the best of cases, answer emails and other correspondence on your behalf in regard to certain issues or certain people, even if it is confidential.

Assistants should not be hired to be eye candy, an audience for your performance, or coffee and lunch delivery persons. The goal is to make them as productive as you are. If you want them to be an executive assistant, compensate them as such, as it pays off in the long run. Indeed, there is an entire cadre of people whose career goal is strictly to be a high-performing executive assistant. They thrive on getting things done for their employer and take great pride in being effective and efficient. Take advantage of that mindset when you interview candidates. Look for the right person who truly loves being an executive assistant.

BALANCE PRINCIPLE 5

Don't let meetings dominate your work time.

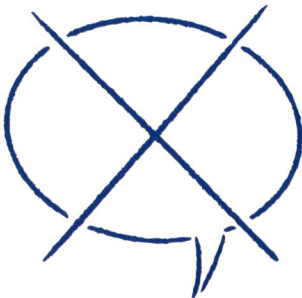

Meetings are the bane of the entrepreneur's life—and if you are a parallel entrepreneur, your entire day can be consumed by a parade of back-to-back meetings. I try not to let that happen to me. While I don't have fixed rules about how long meetings should run, I aim to keep all meetings to 30 minutes and I prefer them not to be booked back-to-back. I would never get any meaningful work done if I did not have several 30-minute breaks between meetings during a day.

But again, you have to be flexible. If a meeting at which your presence has been requested seems not to be a valuable use of your time, you can decline the invitation when you receive it. If a meeting you call appears that it will deserve more time than planned, you can propose to allocate more time to it. Your ultimate goal is to keep every minute of the meetings as productive as possible. You also need to leave time between meetings for phone calls, emails, and thinking time for yourself.

It is critical to good time management to determine what role you need to play in any meeting. Are you the driver of the meeting? Or just a participant? Will attendees be asking you questions that you need to know how to answer? Can you multitask while a virtual meeting is going on, listening in with one ear while doing something else? Since many meetings in today's post-Covid world are still conducted by Zoom, I always look for ways I can multitask when in a meeting if I am not the driver.

BALANCE PRINCIPLE 6

Control your addiction to your phone.

The biggest challenge to balance for any entrepreneur is, without doubt, the phone. I admit that I am "always on." More than vocal phone calls, it is the never-ending stream of text messages, social media posts, and emails that can disrupt your attempts at balance. It is extremely difficult for most people, including me, to control the impulse to check repeatedly for communications and respond to any calls or texts immediately, interrupting whatever you are doing.

Most of us have become addicted to our phones. We feel that we must be in communication with everyone and anyone who sends us a text or an email. Because phone communication is instantaneous, it's easy to think that it just takes a second to stay in touch with others. But by the end of the day, whether you realize it or not, you may have spent several hours of your time texting and emailing. It is both potentially productive and a waste of your precious time.

Social media communication can be a bigger threat. Since more and more people are now posting work-related news, pictures, and short videos on social media, it is inevitable that many of us check our social media accounts during work hours. If you decide to review all these work-related posts and respond frequently, you could easily spend two to three hours a day on social media.

My advice is, link the urgent matters on your calendar to your perception of your phone. Only reply to text messages immediately if their subject is in your urgent category and only check social media posts after work hours. Set aside just five minutes per hour to reply to all non-urgent messages.

Tips for Productivity

1. Invite business associates to brunch on a weekend day for a relaxed meeting to discuss strategy and future planning.

2. Conduct some meetings by asking people to stand during the meeting. This invariably keeps meetings short and actually contributes to greater energy.

3. Ask meeting attendees to give you their questions in advance of the meeting so you can prepare the responses.

4. Go offsite a few times per year for brainstorming sessions. A new environment often provokes new ideas and encourages a sense of freedom to speak.

BALANCE PRINCIPLE 7

Know when to end your day.

Taking control of when to end your day is as important as controlling the start of your day. It takes conscious effort and self-control to curtail the urge to work, especially for parallel entrepreneurs. For some, it may be true that once everyone else leaves the office or logs out, it affords you quiet time to work undisturbed. Staying an extra hour or 90 minutes might be worthwhile on occasion.

But the benefits of working beyond a 10- or 12-hour day every day can be deceiving. Nonstop work becomes inefficient. You tend to lose energy, focus, and clarity. Moreover, if you have a spouse and children, missing dinner and evening time with them can lead to resentment, which can lead to discord and arguments, or even estrangement, in your personal life, which then distracts from your concentration at work.

The benefits of working

beyond a 10- or 12-hour day

every day can be

deceiving. Nonstop work

becomes inefficient.

You tend to

lose energy, focus,

and clarity.

I have learned that I must control my drive and stop work at a reasonable hour. While my executive staff and I often work until 6:00 or even 7:00 pm, I try not to stay much longer on a regular basis. It fatigues me and drains my energy for the next day. Due to urgent matters that always appear, there are exceptions; about once per week, I find I must work until 8:00 or 9:00 p.m. at the office. As that is bound to happen, make sure to stick to a non-overtime schedule as much as possible on all the other days.

The goal of this principle is to have a definitive end of the workday and a definitive beginning of your personal or family time. Think of your day as being a yin-yang analogy.

BALANCE PRINCIPLE 8

Develop habits and routines to manage stress.

As an entrepreneur, especially if you are operating multiple ventures as a parallel entrepreneur, it is possible that your natural psychological makeup may have you well prepared to handle stress. Your native intelligence, naturally high tolerance for risk, energy for an enormous workload, and ability to manage a growing venture are all qualities that make it possible for you to navigate extremely challenging situations without becoming stressed out.

But not all entrepreneurs are built with such resilience to stress. Being unable to effectively manage anxiety, workload pressures, and relationship challenges can derail your path to success. An entrepreneur who cannot counteract stress and keep it from overwhelming his or her ability to calmly approach any situation will not endure the challenges of starting a company.

The reaction is biological, not just psychological. The stress reaction is our evolutionary inheritance to protect us. It triggers the "fight or flight" response. Whenever something is perceived as stressful, the body releases cortisol from the adrenal glands. This hormone increases heart rate, causes cells to produce more fuel for energy, and readies the muscles to either run away from the stressor or take a stance to fight. Either way, the nervous system is alerted and you become anxious, nervous, and either angry or fearful. The stress response triggers your emotions in your limbic system, preventing your prefrontal cortex from analyzing and thinking rationally about how to react to the situation.

Stress takes a toll on your body. It depletes your energy storage, so you ultimately feel exhausted after a stressful period of time. If your entire day is stressful, it is likely that you will become very hungry in the evening and end up eating poorly. You are also likely to sleep poorly, which then causes your body to lack the proper stamina to manage the stresses of the next day. Several stressful days in a row can lead to a vicious circle, whereby biological reactions trigger more stress reactions, thus creating chronic stress. This can lead to "burnout," which can be so debilitating you cannot work in any capacity.

Stress takes a toll on your body. It depletes your energy storage, so you ultimately feel exhausted after a stressful period of time.

John Shen

Take steps to counteract stress, such as meditation.

In short, if you are an entrepreneur whose personality and native abilities to cope with stress are limited, I recommend that you take steps to learn any of the many techniques to counteract your body's natural stress reaction. For instance, you can learn breathing techniques, practice meditation, or create a mantra to recite when you begin to feel the stress reaction occurring in your body. Using techniques like these, you can consciously calm yourself and regain control of your emotional reactions to allow your rational mind to think through problems.

I related the story of my near-suicide and how, during that experience, an email fortuitously revealed the technique that I have since adopted for any type of stressful situation. In this technique, you train yourself to consciously release any negative thoughts, anxiety, and feelings of stress in just one minute. Tell yourself, out loud, to "let it go." It sounds ridiculously simple, but once you train yourself to do this self-talk, it is enormously effective. It can become a habit, an instinctive counteraction to the effects of the fight or flight response.

BALANCE PRINCIPLE 9

Give back to society.

I want to add a last principle to this chapter on balance: the joy of being successful and deciding to spread some of your wealth and generosity to charities that need financial assistance. Being a successful entrepreneur puts you into a special category of people who demonstrate exceptional thinking skills, leadership and management skills, and a grasp of business trends. I believe it behooves you to contribute back to the society that has created the conditions for your success. Our capitalist economy is well structured to reward success with wealth, but at the same time, it often has cracks in it that cause some people to be unable to break through the barriers to success and financial stability.

In my case, I chose to co-found *A Perfect Love Foundation*, which was established by my brother, Steven Shen. This is a charity foundation supporting American families adopting Chinese children with disabilities. Many of these families have financial challenges as they raise these children in the US. The Foundation helps support this unique and valuable cause. Stella and I have made many donations to the Foundation that make the lives of these families better.

In addition, if your entrepreneurial startup proves to be highly successful, I encourage you to give back by supporting future entrepreneurs and investing in their efforts. As you read in the prior chapters, I have long been interested in helping startups. In 2021, during the successful Paycheck Protection Program campaign, ALC made a very good profit from the fees we received from the SBA for helping companies obtain their PPP loans. Later in the year, I decided to create a donor advised fund (DAF) account at National Philanthropic Trust (NPT), a non-profit donation administrator, under the name of "ALC Innovative Ecosystem Fund" and made a $3 million donation to that account. My wife Stella also made a personal $500,000 donation for the same purpose.

Collectively, we allocated a total of $3.5 million to support innovation and entrepreneurship in the nationwide startup community. Monies in this account go out to sponsor and fund many activities in the startup community, for instance, those pitch competitions or demo days at many universities such as California State Universities. Sunstone Management also created a DAF account at NPT in the name of "Sunstone Community Fund" and received $1 million transferred from ALC Innovation Ecosystem Fund this year. Many entrepreneurs and stakeholders in the entrepreneurial ecosystem, especially in California, are becoming beneficiaries of this donation. This is only a start. I will keep donating and funding activities in the future.

I hope you will choose a charity whose cause resonates with you. Providing financial and/or other forms of support will add to your sense of balance in life.

If your entrepreneurial

startup proves to

be highly successful,

I encourage you to give

back by supporting future

entrepreneurs and

investing

in their efforts.

FIRST-GENERATION ENTREPRENEURS: SPECIAL ISSUES REGARDING BALANCE

Although first-generation immigrant entrepreneurs often come from countries that have close-knit family systems, such as China and India, the drive to succeed can make them lose sight of the importance of balancing their work life with their personal life. They often believe they must make great sacrifices in order to achieve the American Dream, even if it includes less quality time with their extended family. To assimilate, they buy into the American culture that does not honor as strongly as many other cultures the value of multi-generational families living with each other or nearby. First-generation entrepreneurs will stay at the office late at night and get there early in the morning, as I did for years, failing to recognize the toll it takes on close-knit families.

Another common issue regarding balance for first-generation entrepreneurs is disregard of the importance of staying healthy. Here too, while chasing the American Dream, they may also buy into a version of American culture that includes fast-food lunches, eating at your desk, failing to exercise, and not managing one's stress levels with some time off to rest and regroup. I confess that I have not taken an extended vacation in many years, not longer than a few days. I own a beautiful catamaran sailboat, but I cannot skipper it and so I only use it for business meetings. I have found it difficult to give myself the leeway to take time off, being as driven and busy as I am with all my companies. So I give this advice knowing that I must soon follow it myself. If you are a first-generation immigrant entrepreneur, take at least a week off once per year to reinvigorate yourself, breathe, and renew your appreciation for life.

John Shen

REFLECTIONS ON THIS CHAPTER

Consider these questions. Write out your answers or identify a "success buddy" such as a business partner, another entrepreneur, or a spouse or friend with whom you can discuss the questions.

- How are you handling the balance of your work and home life? What is your philosophy of balance and are you managing it well?

- Are you living a healthy lifestyle or are you heading towards unhealthy habits?

- Do you have an assistant and are you relying on him or her to help you be productive?

- What activities do you do to prevent stress from overwhelming you?

- Do you work with your spouse? What limits do you have on discussing work issues at home?

Is Parallel Entrepreneurship for You?

John Shen

At this juncture in my career, I have come to revel in being a parallel entrepreneur. When I arise in the morning, I am as excited to look over my portfolio of companies as a sea captain readying their ship for sailing into the unknown waters of daring future adventures.

And as a final reminder, you do not need to have been born to be an entrepreneur. You can develop the eight necessary talents that I have defined in this book.

1. Drive and ambition
2. Ability to capitalize on opportunity
3. Resilience
4. Long-term risk-taking
5. Strategic thinking
6. Financial savvy
7. Leadership and vision
8. Balance

I am not saying it is easy. Being a parallel entrepreneur means crossing a lot more swamps. I will be the first to admit that running multiple businesses simultaneously is not for everyone. Some people must focus hard on leading and growing one single business at a time. They might even desire to develop a single business into a far larger enterprise than any of my companies are at this time. Or perhaps they may be seeking to go multinational, taking their business into dozens of countries around the world. Every entrepreneur has to decide for themselves, of course, how they can best lead their company and, consequently, how many businesses they want to operate at a time.

My closing message, however, is that if you are looking to become an entrepreneur or are already involved in a startup, allow yourself to dream bigger than you might have. This is a new era for entrepreneurship. As this book has demonstrated, there are incredible, valuable benefits to launching and innovating multiple companies simultaneously. Here is a summary of many advantages of being a parallel entrepreneur, which this book has highlighted:

1 ***Diversification of your income sources.*** Here's an analogy worth considering. When you invest money in a savings or retirement account, you usually diversify your investment in a broad-based portfolio of stocks, bonds, and other investment instruments, right? The same needs to be true for your entrepreneurial ventures. Running a business is just like investing. You are investing your time, money, and passion. So why not think of your entrepreneurship using the same portfolio concept. Don't put everything in a single opportunity. Diversify across different opportunities with your allocated time, money, and energy. If you have four or five different businesses, each one has a chance to succeed. It's like having a really good portfolio.

Like investments, statistically speaking, each business has a certain chance of succeeding. Some businesses are riskier than others that are more conservative. This suggests that you might look to create a portfolio of businesses at various risk levels. One or two may succeed at different levels of payoffs, while another may fail. But in the long run, any losses you have can be offset by the winning ventures. You may even hit a home run with one business that turns into a "unicorn," meaning something rare: a business that makes you hundreds of millions of dollars.

2 ***Greater learning potential that can expand your opportunities and improve your 8 entrepreneurial talents.*** When you have multiple businesses,

John Shen

you are exposed to a wider horizon of trends from which you can identify opportunities you might be able to capitalize on. The executive teams you have managing all your companies are also a valuable cadre of people from whom you can learn. Each may have different leadership styles that can inform your own. They bring different experiences and backgrounds into your companies, which facilitates and enriches mutual learning. This cross-board learning enables you to see things from many different angles. It's an internal network effect.

Sharing resources for cost savings. Given that all businesses need a variety of resources, there are huge financial savings to be had when you operate multiple companies and share those resources. These range from legal and accounting departments to IT and HR. Moreover, any time a business needs a specialized consultant, it is likely that one of your other businesses may already be using that very consultant. You can spend less time finding and vetting that consultant or company before hiring them.

Challenge and Excitement. This is perhaps what I consider the greatest benefit of being a parallel entrepreneur simultaneously operating multiple companies. While at times your work may seem stressful, it is more likely that, like me, you find your life becoming ever more stimulating, exciting, and full of happiness—more than you ever imagined possible. Your creativity and intellect will challenge you to work hard and excel. Your knowledge of the industries in which you participate will expand, and your growing network of connections will bring you into contact with fascinating CEOs, executives, and even political people in your city or town.

FIRST-GENERATION ENTREPRENEURS: CLOSING ADVICE

I also have a summary of my recommendations for readers of this book who, like me, are first-generation immigrant entrepreneurs.

Always be prepared to face hurdles as an outsider. From learning to speak English like an American to dealing with the federal government to obtain your green card, you will face myriad hurdles. It simply helps to remember that becoming an entrepreneur will not be easy for you as a first-generation immigrant. Not being surprised or shocked that you have to cross swamps that natural-born citizens do not face can go a long way to decreasing your stress. Just expect that life will not be as easy for you, but your blessing is that you are in the United States where the American Dream is yours to capture.

The most difficult hurdles you face are the ones inside you. I know from my own experience that when you are born and raised outside of the USA, you have grown up with a very different mindset. Your native culture may be vastly alien to how Americans think and act. What this means, though, is that many of the most difficult hurdles are the ones inside you. They come from your own upbringing, which influenced your psychological makeup and perceptions of how society works. But these are changeable; you can learn to overcome a mindset that interferes with your progress. In my case, I had to learn to overcome being a shy, introverted student from China, whose native culture discouraged ambition, standing

out in the crowd, and trying to innovate business and society. It took years for me to develop a more American mindset that allowed me to unleash my natural drive. I am sure you too can do it.

Your native country may prove to be an element in your business success. While you may be trying to forget where you came from, keep in mind that your native country might represent a market you can mine for new business. Remember, you have the advantage of knowing the language, the geography, the people, and the culture of your native land. I have been quite fortunate in that several of my companies have succeeded by being able to find large client bases among Chinese families who want to emigrate to the US as well as the large Chinese communities in the southern California area. You too may find opportunities for your entrepreneurial endeavor among your compatriots in the United States.

America is a melting pot. Finally, always keep in mind that the USA has a long history of being one of the most diverse countries in the world because it has accepted waves and waves of immigrants for hundreds of years. You are not in a unique position fighting an uphill battle to be accepted. Millions of others have come to America and become integrated into the fabric of American society. And thousands of immigrants have become successful entrepreneurs, business owners, and political leaders despite not having been born in this country. You are becoming part of the history of the United States, and the generations of your family that follow you will always look back and thank you for coming here.

America is indeed a melting pot and our diverse cultural heritages are increasingly recognized. For example, at the invitation of President Joe Biden and the First Lady, Dr. Jill Biden, Stella and I attended the *First Ever* Lunar New Year reception held in the White House, on Thursday, January 26, 2023. The Lunar New Year is the most celebrated festival in China and in many East and Southeast Asian countries. President and Dr. Biden are the first Presidential family to host an official celebrative reception at the White House in observance of this event. We were so proud to be part of the small group of guests at the White House.

Wishing You Luck

Parallel entrepreneurship may not be for everyone, but my guess is that we will see a lot more of it in the coming years, as very successful individual entrepreneurs realize that they, too, have the attributes to launch and operate more than a single business at a time. I hope my own journey has inspired you and that my advice for developing the eight talents in this book will prepare you for a rewarding and successful future.

My best regards,
John Shen

ACKNOWLEDGMENTS

I am extremely grateful for the contributions of so many people in the evolution and development of this book.

First and foremost, since the book covers so much of my life journey, I extend my deepest appreciation for all my family members who offered incredible support over the last half century. Many of them have made a profound impact on my life. I want to recognize and thank each one of them.

I would first like to acknowledge the immense contributions of my wife, Stella Zhang. She has been my rock, my support system, and my best business partner in every aspect of my life in the last decade. Her love, care, and commitment have been instrumental in helping me become the person I am today. She is also a great leader and manager. Her business acumen, strategic thinking, and unwavering determination have been invaluable to the success of all my businesses, especially American Lending Center. Her dedication and tireless work ethic have not only inspired me but have also set a high standard for our team. I am proud to work alongside her and to share in the fruits of our labor. I am truly grateful to have her by my side, and I cannot imagine my life without her. She is a true blessing.

My father was a professor teaching Chinese Classical Literature at Peking University. He authored and co-authored a handful of professional books and taught thousands of college students during his career. However, what truly made him proud, as he admitted many times when he was alive, were his two sons. He passed away after a battle with cancer in 2010. Despite facing immense physical and emotional pain, he never lost his positive spirit and continued to inspire me with his strength and courage. He was always there for me, offering his love, guidance, and support whenever I needed it. He taught us the value of hard work, perseverance, and humility, and his legacy will live on through the countless lives he touched.

I also thank my mother, who has always been an outstanding mother and a productive high school teacher throughout her career. Her selflessness, caring nature, and unwavering dedication to our family have been a constant source of inspiration to me. I am grateful for her love and guidance. Thank you, Mom, for all that you do and for being the amazing person that you are.

My brother Steven is a successful businessman and passionate leader in what he does. He has been one of my most ardent supporters over the years. My two sons, Ryan and Leo, both in college now, bring so much joy, laughter, and love into my life. They are both unique individuals with their own strengths, interests, and personalities, and I am constantly amazed by their growth and development. I am grateful to be able to watch them learn and flourish. Their mother, my ex-wife Wanshuang, offered patience, kindness, and care to Ryan and Leo. I appreciate her support, too. I love all my family members more than words can express.

Secondly, this book is mainly about entrepreneurship. I want to recognize and thank all my business partners, employees, clients, and anyone else who made my business successful.

My real estate business failed in 2008. I learned so much from the failure. For those with whom I worked in that business, I cannot name each one of them, but I want to sincerely apologize, but also thank you for being on my side, supporting me without reservation when I was in such a tough situation.

When I bounced back and launched a new business in 2009, I was fortunate enough to build a much more sustainable business model. In the early years of American Lending Center, my partner Bruce Thompson, among others, brought strong leadership to the business. Bruce, Queena Zhao, Leo Zhou, and Stella became the best management team partners I have ever had. As I launched more businesses in the following years, Daniel Wheeler, Adam Carrillo, John Keisler, and others joined me and took over the management of Sunstone Trust Company, Partake Collective, and Sunstone Management. In many ways, these people mentored and challenged me constantly to be the best I could be. I want to recognize the contribution these business partners have made to my entrepreneurial career. Their own amazing accomplishments have provided great inspiration for me. Moreover, on numerous occasions, they showed me that I can achieve beyond expectations, no matter the circumstances. They have collectively demonstrated that everyone can make the impossible possible!

I want to thank every employee my business has ever hired. Because of my employees' efforts, I have been able to positively impact the lives of thousands of people. I will be forever grateful to Sirena Wang, Chingy Norton, Candice Lam, Gino Zhao, Nathan Jia, Jasmine Jiang, Aeson Chen, Kiki Zhao, and many others who joined me in the early years for their significant contributions to my business and professional life. As I faced many challenges in the fast-growing phase of my business, Justin Blackhall, Scott Wagner, Scott Thompson among many others stepped up. They never stopped inspiring me and eventually guided me through the dark times of the wild industry of EB-5.

Last, but not least, I must acknowledge all those who have contributed to the publication of this book. Los Angeles editor and writer, Rick Benzel, did the heaviest lifting. He had the tough job of molding, shaping, and editing my original writing and re-writes into the final product that would effectively inspire and inform the reader. Rick and I had many in-depth discussions about both content and style. I think we both can be proud of the result of our efforts. Julie Simpson put the finishing touches on the book with her excellent copyediting skills.

My publisher, Susan Shankin, created a marvelous cover and interior design that transformed the manuscript into a beautiful and readable book. Tim Kummerow prepared the artwork illustrations on many pages. I appreciate the great job Susan and Tim have done.

As you have read in this book, all great achievements are a team effort. The people I have acknowledged were significant team members who contributed to this book. I am thankful I have had the opportunity to work with each of them.

ABOUT THE AUTHOR

JOHN SHEN (né Zhong Shen) is the founder and Chairman of the Board of four currently operating companies headquartered in Irvine, CA. He is a visionary thinker about innovation and entrepreneuring. He has coined the term "parallel entrepreneur," referring to entrepreneurs who, like himself, choose to launch and operate multiple companies simultaneously.

John grew up in China and earned his undergraduate degree from Peking University Law School in 1992. He emigrated to the US in 1993 as a foreign student and earned a master's degree in Statistics and Decision Sciences from Duke University in 1996. He changed his name to John Z. Shen when he became a US citizen in 2009. His wife, Stella Zhang, is his business partner. John has two sons, Ryan Shen and Leo Shen.

John views his career as an entrepreneur as being divided into three phases: Entrepreneurship 1.0. (2004–2009) in which he founded and ran real estate brokerage, mortgage brokerage, and property management companies in Orlando, Florida; Entrepreneurship 2.0 (2010–2017) in which he founded and ran three companies, two in the private lending and investment industry and one in the hotel/resort industry; and Entrepreneurship 3.0 (2017–present) in which he became a true "parallel entrepreneur" by launching two more companies—a licensed trust company and a ghost/virtual kitchen company.

John's path to being a parallel entrepreneur began in 2010, when he founded American Lending Center (ALC) in 2009, a small startup that he conceived, led, and transformed into one of the most successful nonbank small business lending institutions in the US. ALC represents an innovation in financial engineering, by merging the federal government's EB-5 program that seeks to attract foreign investment into the US, with the Small Business Administration (SBA) 504 program, which co-funds loans with banks to assist small businesses and create jobs. ALC has become a leading nonbank entity in the EB-5 space, operating nationwide throughout all fifty states of the US to funnel foreign investment into US small businesses. ALC was one of the most productive Paycheck Protection Program (PPP) lenders during the Covid-19 pandemic and is an approved lender for the SBA 7(a) program and the State Small Business Credit Initiative (SSBCI) program in California.

In 2012, John and his partners purchased 360 acres of raw land and developed a lakefront hotel and vineyards, Eritage Resort, in Walla Walla, Washington. After a five-year development and construction period, Eritage opened in 2017 and helped Walla Walla rank as one of "The 50 Best Places to Travel in 2018" by *Travel + Leisure* magazine.

Since 2015, John has founded three other dynamic startups—a diversified investment firm, Sunstone Management (SMI), a "TrustTech" company, Sunstone Trust Company (STC), and a "virtual kitchen/food hall" developer and operator, Partake Collective (Partake), all reflecting John's innovative business thinking.

His entrepreneurial vision and leadership helped propel his companies on a fast track to success. Both ALC and Sunstone Management were listed among "America's Fastest Growing Companies" by Financial Times in 2021–2023. ALC was included in the Inc. 5000 "Fastest Growing Private Companies" in 2020–2023, and Sunstone in 2020–2022.

John possesses a great passion for encouraging and sponsoring startups and small businesses. He is one of the three co-founders of the

Long Beach Accelerator. This is the first startup accelerator built on a public-private-education partnership. John served on the inaugural board and has been an honorary board member since November 2021.

John is widely recognized by many professional networks for his support of entrepreneuring startups and respected in his communities as a financial engineer, a visionary, and a leader in business operation and virtual kitchen development, among other fields. Among the notable awards and accolades he has received are: California Financial Services Executive of the Year and also Man of the Year in the field of finance by *Top 100 Registry* (2023), Distinguished Leader in Wealth Management by the *Orange County Business Journal* (2022), Orange County Visionary by the *Los Angeles Times* (2022 and 2023), the Albert Nelson Marquis Lifetime Achievement Award by Marquis *Who's Who* (2021), and Coleman's SBA 504 Lender of the Year Award (2017). John has been a passionate volunteer for Duke University's Alumni Admissions Advisory Committee (AAAC) in China since 2013. He earned the Forever Duke Award in 2015, and in 2016 he established a unique endowment fund to help the international recruitment of students to Duke University.

Follow John's journey at
www.crossingtheswamp.com